Kid-First
Co-Parenting

They See You, They Hear You, They Love You

Dr. Cindy H. Carr, D.Min. MACL

This book is published by **CHC Connect**.

All views and opinions expressed in this work are those of the author. Any errors or omissions are unintentional.

Printed in the United States of America
First Edition, 2026

ISBN: 978-1-971192-11-6

For permissions or inquiries, contact:
Cindy H. Carr
cindyhcarr@outlook.com
www.cindyhcarr.com

Acknowledgments

This book exists because of children who lived inside adult conflict they did not create, adapted too early, and deserved steadier ground. They are the quiet teachers behind every page. I am grateful to parents, caregivers, and professionals who have trusted me with their stories. Your courage, honesty, and persistence shaped this work. Though your stories appear in composite form, your wisdom lives in these pages.

To the counselors, clinicians, pastors, educators, and family advocates who labor beside families in complicated seasons, thank you for holding the tension between compassion and clarity, mercy and truth. Your steady presence shaped how this book was written and why. To friends and colleagues who read drafts, asked hard questions, and refined the language and heart of this work, thank you. You helped keep this book gentle and grounded.

Finally, to God, near to the brokenhearted and steady in the chaos, thank You for patience to write slowly, wisdom to choose clarity over noise, and grace to believe steady love shapes lives, even in imperfect stories.

Table of Contents

How to Use This Book

Quick Start: If This Is Your Situation, Start Here

- If safety is uncertain (injuries, threats, unsafe supervision): start with the safety-related chapters and go directly to Appendix I. Get local professional guidance.

If you feel behind, ashamed, or exhausted: take a breath. We don't fix the past by punishing ourselves—we build a safer future by starting now.

- If conflict is constant and communication keeps exploding: start with the chapters on conflict exposure, lanes (cordial/parallel/protective), and communication tools; use Appendix C for scripts.

- If transitions are the hardest part: start with the transition chapter(s) and use Appendix B and Appendix F.

- If you are the steady caregiver and resentment is growing: start with the capacity-gap and village chapters; use Appendix D for regulation tools and Appendix F for weekly stability planning.

- If your child is anxious, angry, or shutting down: start with the chapters on regulation, co-regulation, and emotion coaching; then use Appendix D and Appendix F.

- If you are building a village (grandparents/kinship/blended support): start with the village chapters; use Appendix G (plan template) and Appendix K (group guide).

You don't have to read straight through. Many parents read by pain point. Use this map to start where your child needs help most.

This book is written in full paragraphs, with varied rhythm, and a warm, direct voice because overwhelmed families do not need a workbook—they need a steady guide.

Each chapter includes some combination of: a short real-life moment, a kid-first reframe, a simple framework, short scripts you can actually say, a reset practice, and—when appropriate—a brief prayer.

You can read the book straight through, or you can begin where your family is hurting most.

A Word About Research, Language, and Citations

This is a faith-rooted book written for the real world. But it is also written to be responsible and recommendable by therapists, pastors, and counselors.

So when we make claims about children, stress, discipline, conflict exposure, and family dynamics, we will cite the research—prioritizing clinical guidelines and meta-analyses where possible.

Style note: We use APA 7th edition formatting in the back matter References. To keep the reading experience warm and uncluttered, most citations appear as chapter endnotes.

Language note: We avoid diagnosing or labeling adults. When we describe hard situations, we name the child's reality—what is observable and what impacts safety and stability—rather than assigning clinical categories.

A Gentle Safety Note
If a child may be experiencing abuse, neglect, unsafe supervision, or credible threat, seek immediate professional help through appropriate channels in your location. If this is an emergency, call your local emergency number.

The goal is not escalation or accusation—it is protection, clarity, and a steady response that keeps the child safe. Kid-first always begins with safety.

Blessing for the Work Ahead

God, help us keep the main thing the main thing.

Give us courage to choose peace over power, wisdom over reactivity, and stability over chaos.

Teach us to honor people with dignity while also telling the truth and setting boundaries that protect what is sacred.

And give our children the gift of growing up unburdened—held, seen, and safe.

Amen.

Front Matter Endnotes (APA 7th Edition)

1. van Eldik, W. M., Luijk, M. P. C. M., Parry, L. Q., & Prinzie, P. (2020). The interparental relationship: Meta-analytic associations with children's maladjustment and responses to interparental conflict. Psychological Bulletin, 146(7), 553–594. https://doi.org/10.1037/bul0000233

2. Schrodt, P. (2025). Interparental conflict and parent–child triangulation: A meta-analytical review of children feeling caught between parents. Human Communication Research Advance online publication. https://doi.org/10.1093/hcr/hqaf018

3. Association of Family and Conciliation Courts. (2019). Guidelines for parenting coordination. https://www.afccnet.org/Portals/0/Committees/Gu idelines%20for%20Parenting%20Coordination%20 2019.pdf

4. Sege, R. D., & Siegel, B. S.; Council on Child Abuse and Neglect; Committee on Psychosocial Aspects of Child and Family Health. (2018). Effective discipline to raise healthy children. Pediatrics, 142(6), e20183112. https://doi.org/10.1542/peds.2018-3112

Introduction

A Note From the Author

If you are reading this, there is a good chance you are tired.

Tired of trying to "do it right" while your family story keeps shifting. Tired of hard conversations that turn sideways. Tired of watching a child absorb tension they did not create—and should never have to carry.

This book is for the parent or caregiver who wants to stop bleeding adult stress into childhood.

It's for the steady ones—the ones who keep showing up, even when others cannot. It's also for the ones who want to show up better, but keep finding themselves hijacked by fear, old pain, and reactivity. And it's for the pastors, counselors, mentors, and clinicians who walk beside families and quietly think, There has to be a clearer way forward than this.

There is.

Not perfect. Not easy. But clearer. Kinder. Steadier.

The Promise of This Book

Kid-First Co-Parenting helps adults move from conflict and confusion into clarity and a workable plan—so children are not carrying what adults haven't resolved.

Sometimes that plan includes real collaboration. Sometimes it simply means predictable structure and low-conflict boundaries. Either way, the goal is the same: children are not carrying what adults haven't resolved.

Sometimes that cooperation will be between two active parents. Sometimes it will be between a parent and grandparents. Sometimes it will be a "village" of caregivers who share responsibility because one person cannot hold it all.

And sometimes, cooperation won't be possible.

Even then, stability is.

Kid-first co-parenting is not about controlling other adults. It's about leading yourself, building structure where it's needed, and protecting the child's nervous system from adult chaos.

Who This Book Is For

This book is written for parents and caregivers raising children across two homes, one home, blended systems, or kinship care.

It's for the "cleanup crew" caregiver who keeps picking up the pieces—and is fighting anger, bitterness, or exhaustion because of it.

It's for families with uneven capacity, where one adult carries more emotional steadiness, follow-through, or responsibility.

A quick definition: capacity is not character. It is a caregiver's current ability to provide safe supervision, emotional steadiness, and consistent follow-through. Capacity can rise with treatment, support, and time—and it can drop during crisis. Kid-first planning responds to reality without shaming anyone.

It's for high-conflict situations where communication escalates quickly and children are regularly exposed to adult tension.

And it's for pastors, counselors, clinicians, and mentors who want a child-centered, practical framework to recommend.

What This Book Is Not
This is not a memoir.

I will include short, purposeful stories at times—usually composite vignettes drawn from common family experiences—but the spotlight stays on the reader: the parent, caregiver, and child.

This is also not a legal manual or a substitute for professional care. When safety is at risk—physical harm, neglect, threats, unsafe supervision, or credible fear—your next step is not "better communication." Your next step is protection and appropriate professional involvement.

The Heart of Kid-First Co-Parenting
There is a quiet truth that changes everything:

Children do not need perfect adults. They need regulated adults. They need steady adults. They need protected space to be children.

That means the adults do the adult work—so the child doesn't have to.

Kid-first parenting does not require that every adult is equally healthy, equally mature, or equally cooperative. It requires that at least one caregiver is willing to build stability on purpose.

The Three Pathways: Cordial, Parallel, Protective

Not every family can "co-parent" in the same way at the same time. Pretending otherwise often creates more harm. So we choose the healthiest pathway for the child right now:

Not every family can co-parent the same way in every season. In this book, you'll learn three practical 'lanes'—cordial, parallel, and protective—so you can choose the healthiest pathway for your child right now.

Honor Without Denial

A central tension in messy family systems is capacity. There are seasons when a parent or caregiver cannot show up consistently—because of illness, addiction, instability, or a nervous system that is simply not steady.

Kid-first wisdom refuses a false choice: honoring someone does not mean ignoring reality or sacrificing safety. It means telling the truth with love, setting wise boundaries, and creating stability where it is possible.

We will not recruit the child into adult resentment. We will process adult grief in adult places. We will protect the child's heart while protecting the child's safety.

Chapter 1
Kid-First Co-Parenting
Starts Here

Mercy Moment

If your family story feels messy, hear this clearly: it is not too late, and you are not disqualified. You can have mercy for yourself without excusing harm. You can tell the truth about what happened without letting guilt run your future.

Shame paralyzes. Mercy mobilizes. We start from where we are, with what we have, and we learn the skills that build a steadier home from here forward.

Keep the Main Thing the Main Thing

Here is the win: children feel loved, safe, and protected—and adult problems are not bleeding over onto them.

Children tend to interpret adult tension as danger—even when no one raises their voice. When parents carry unresolved conflict, children often carry the anxiety.

Most parents don't need more pressure. You're already carrying enough. What you need is a way forward that feels clear and doable—especially when parenting has become complicated.

Kid-first co-parenting is not about building a perfect home. It's about building a stable one.

Because children can handle a lot of realities when they are anchored in safety and predictability. What they struggle to handle is adult instability— when conflict becomes the atmosphere, when moods become the weather, and when they feel responsible for keeping the peace.

So before we talk about tactics—bedtime, discipline, screens, schedules—we start with the foundation: children should not have to carry what adults haven't resolved.

That sentence is not meant to shame you. It's meant to free you. It gives you a simple question to return to when emotions rise: Does what I'm about to do build stability—or increase chaos?

Research consistently finds that ongoing interparental conflict is associated with increased risk for children's emotional and behavioral difficulties, as well as heightened stress responses. The point is not to blame parents; it is to name the cost to children so we can choose a better pattern together.1

What Kid-First Co-Parenting Is (and Isn't)
Kid-first does not mean adult-last. It does not mean children run the home. It does not mean you

ignore boundaries, consequences, or wise authority.

Kid-first means the child's safety and stability become the filter for every adult decision—even when adult feelings are loud.

It means we stop asking, Who's right? and start asking, What protects peace for the child?

Kid-first also doesn't require a traditional two-parent structure. Some families are raising children with grandparents, extended family, or a small "village" of support. Some children have one consistently present caregiver. In those stories, kid-first co-parenting becomes kid-first caregiving: the adults who are available agree on stability, structure, and dignity.

And here is a gentle, important truth: you don't have to agree on the reasons to agree on the plan. You can be compassionate about why an adult struggles and still build a structure that keeps the child safe.

Team Before Tactics
Most conflict between caregivers isn't really about the child. It's about what the child represents: control, fear, shame, loyalty, old wounds, and unspoken expectations.

But children do not experience your intentions. They experience your environment.

That's why the order matters. Team first, tactics second. Alignment first, discipline second. Relationship first, rules second.

"Team" does not always mean close partnership. In high-conflict situations, "team" can mean a structured agreement: one communication channel, one predictable schedule, one set of non-negotiables that protect the child's nervous system.

When children feel caught between adults—forced to take sides, carry messages, or manage emotions—their sense of safety fractures. They learn to edit themselves. They learn to perform loyalty. They learn to hide what they feel. Our job is to keep them out of the middle.2

Regulation Is Leadership
If there is one skill that changes a home faster than any parenting technique, it is emotional regulation.

Not the kind where you pretend you're fine. The kind where you recognize, I'm activated, and you choose steadiness anyway.

Children borrow regulation before they build it. They learn calm by living near it. They learn repair by watching it. So kid-first co-parenting means the adults practice becoming the safest nervous systems in the room—steady, grounded, and willing to return when we miss it.

Here is what regulation looks like in real life:

• Pausing before you respond—especially to a text, tone, or triggering moment.

• Naming the moment honestly: I'm getting worked up. I need a minute.

• Choosing a next step that lowers conflict exposure for the child, even if it doesn't satisfy your pride.

Leadership is not loud. It is steady.

And steadiness is one of the most protective gifts you can give a child.

The First Skill: A 60-Second Kid-First Pause
When tension rises, decisions get rushed. This is where families spiral—because the adult nervous system goes into fight, flight, freeze, or fawn, and the child is left to absorb the fallout.

Use this 30–60 second pause before texting, reacting, or making changes:

1) What is happening right now (fact, not interpretation)?

2) What is the child experiencing because of this?

3) What am I feeling—and what am I afraid will happen?

4) What decision would build stability and reduce chaos?

This pause is not weakness. It is spiritual maturity and emotional leadership in real time.

Simple Scripts
You don't need the perfect speech. You need a few phrases that keep you kind, clear, and child-centered.

To the other caregiver (cordial): "For the child's sake, I'd like us to keep this calm and clear. Here's what I'm proposing…"

To the other caregiver (parallel): "I'm going to keep communication brief and focused on logistics. Please send updates by text/email."

To yourself (when activated): "Pause. Lead. Protect the child. Return regulated."

To a child (age-appropriate): "Both of your parents love you. Sometimes adults have hard seasons that can feel confusing. My job is to make sure you are safe, cared for, and never alone in this."

To extended family: "We're choosing what supports the child's stability right now. We welcome help and encouragement—not pressure."

A Small Step This Week
For the next seven days, choose one small, stabilizing action you can repeat.

• Make one predictable routine sacred (bedtime, school morning, dinner).

• Choose one communication boundary (time of day you respond; one channel; no conflict within earshot of the child).

• Do one repair the same day you miss it: "I'm sorry. I raised my voice. That wasn't your responsibility."

Small decisions, repeated faithfully, build a home a child can breathe in.

Closing Prayer
God, help me keep the main thing the main thing.

Give me wisdom to build stability and love for these children, even when the adults are strained, wounded, or divided.

Teach me to honor people with dignity while also telling the truth and setting boundaries that protect what is sacred.

Give me courage to choose peace over power, and faith to believe that steady love can shape a legacy—even in a complicated story.

Amen.

Kid-First takeaway: the win is a child who feels loved, safe, and protected—while adult problems stay in adult hands.

Chapter 1 Endnotes (APA 7th Edition)

1. van Eldik, W. M., Luijk, M. P. C. M., Parry, L. Q., & Prinzie, P. (2020). The interparental relationship: Meta-analytic associations with children's maladjustment and responses to interparental conflict. Psychological Bulletin, 146(7), 553–594. https://doi.org/10.1037/bul0000233

2. Schrodt, P. (2025). Interparental conflict and parent–child triangulation: A meta-analytical review of children feeling caught between parents. Human Communication Research. Advance online publication. https://doi.org/10.1093/hcr/hqaf018

3. Association of Family and Conciliation Courts. (2019). Guidelines for parenting coordination. https://www.afccnet.org/Portals/0/Committees/Gu idelines%20for%20Parenting%20Coordination%20 2019.pdf

Chapter 2
Regulation Is Leadership

When adults can stay grounded, children can stay children.

Some chapters in a co-parenting story are loud: court dates, custody changes, family meetings, hard conversations in parking lots. But the chapters that shape a child's nervous system are often quiet. They're written in tone. In facial expression. In the way we breathe when we're angry. In the way we choose our words when we're tired. Children don't just listen to what we say. They listen to who we are while we say it.

When a child moves between homes, the transition is not only logistical. It is biological. Their body is scanning: Is it safe here? Do I need to be on guard? Am I about to be caught in the middle? If adults are dysregulated—escalating, blaming, spiraling, slamming doors—children will adjust by becoming smaller, louder, or hyper-responsible. Not because they're "bad," but because their system is trying to survive.

Kid-first co-parenting begins with a simple truth: your regulation is part of your child's environment.1 When you bring steadiness, you are giving your child a gift no schedule can replace—a nervous system that has room to learn, play, and grow.

Your Nervous System Sets the Temperature

Most conflict is not really about the calendar. It's about threat. When people feel threatened, they move into protection: control, attack, shutdown, avoidance. Polyvagal research describes how our bodies read cues of safety and cues of danger, often before our minds can explain what's happening.1 That means a co-parenting conversation can be "about pick-up time," but your body is responding as if it's about abandonment, betrayal, humiliation, or fear.

Here's the hard part: children don't have the power to leave the room. They can't say, "I'll be back when you're regulated." They absorb the atmosphere and adapt themselves to it. Over time, the child learns what kind of world they live in: predictable or volatile, safe or unstable, repairable or fragile.

Regulation is not pretending you're fine. Regulation is noticing what is happening in you and choosing a response that protects what is sacred—your child's safety and belonging. It is leadership with a calm spine and a soft heart.

Why You Lose Your Words When You're Triggered

In stress, the brain shifts. Research on stress and the prefrontal cortex shows that high stress can rapidly weaken the brain's "top-down" functions—planning, flexibility, impulse control—while strengthening more reflexive emotional and habitual responses.23 In plain language: when you feel threatened, your wise mind can go offline and your survival mind can take the wheel.

That is why you can be a thoughtful adult at 10:00 a.m. and a sharp, reactive version of yourself at 8:30 p.m. That is why you can believe in peace—and still feel your chest tighten when a certain text comes through. Regulation is not about willpower; it's about wiring and practice.

This also means something important for co-parenting: if you wait until you're flooded to "try to communicate better," you will keep failing. Not because you're hopeless, but because your brain is not built to do complex cooperation while it believes it's under threat.23 We have to build a plan for the moments when our best self is unavailable.

The Age of the Wound

Many caregivers are shocked by how young they can feel in conflict. You're talking about a child's backpack, but inside you feel five years old—unseen, blamed, or panicked. You're negotiating a holiday schedule, but your body is bracing like you're back in a season where you had no control.

Trauma theory reminds us that intense experiences can be stored not only as facts we remember but as body-based states we relive—tight throat, racing heart, shutting down, rage, collapse.7 When that state is activated, you may react from the age you were when you first learned, "I am not safe," or "I will be abandoned," or "No one is coming."

This matters because co-parenting conflict often touches the oldest places in us: attachment wounds, shame stories, powerlessness, betrayal. If we don't learn to recognize our regressions, we will keep handing our child the bill for pain we never paid.

Compassion is not a pass. It's a pathway. The moment you can say, "I feel younger right now," you create space between feeling and action. That space is where prayer, skill, and wisdom can do their work.

Co-Regulation: How Children Borrow Calm Until They Can Build It

Children are not born with mature self-regulation. They develop it through relationships. A major practice brief on co-regulation describes it as an interactive process in which supportive adults provide warmth, structure, and coaching so children can learn to manage emotions and behavior across development.4 A multilevel review likewise defines coregulation between parent and child as coordination of biological and behavioral systems that supports the development of the child's own regulatory systems.5

In other words, children learn regulation in the presence of regulated adults. This is why kid-first co-parenting can't be reduced to "be nice." A child's brain is learning what to do with stress by watching what you do with stress.

And here's the truth for messy families: co-regulation can come from a parent, a grandparent, a foster parent, an aunt, a coach, a teacher, a godparent. Sometimes it really does take a village. What matters is that the child has at least one steady nervous system to borrow.

A Simple Regulation Plan for Co-Parents
This is not a workbook, but I want to give you something you can actually use when life is loud. A regulation plan is not for your best day. It's for your worst day—the day you're exhausted, triggered, and tempted to win instead of protect.

Below are four "micro-skills" that change everything. They are small enough to do, even in messy systems. They are also powerful enough to shift the emotional climate your child lives in.

1) Name the State, Not the Story

Before you argue about facts, name your state. State language sounds like: "I'm getting flooded." "I'm starting to feel defensive." "My body is tense." Story language sounds like: "You always do this." "You don't care." "You're trying to control me."

State language keeps you honest without escalating. It is also a quiet form of discipleship: you are refusing to bear false witness about someone's motives, and you are taking responsibility for your own inner world.

Script to the other parent: "I want to keep this calm for the child. I'm feeling activated. I'm going to pause and come back at 6:00."

2) Create a 90-Second Reset

When stress hits, your body needs a moment to downshift. A short reset helps your physiology catch up with your values. Try this:

• Put both feet on the ground. Exhale longer than you inhale (for example, inhale 4 seconds, exhale 6).

• Relax your jaw. Drop your shoulders. Unclench your hands.

• Say a brief prayer that fits in one breath: "Lord, make me steady."

Then decide your next right step. The goal is not to feel nothing; it's to respond like a grown-up who is protecting a child.

3) Build a "No-Conflict Zone" Around Transitions

Hand-offs are sacred ground. They are not the place to hash out old pain or prove a point. If you want a child to transition well, keep the atmosphere low-drama and predictable.

A helpful rule: no conflict within earshot of the child, and no conflict within one hour of a transition when possible. This boundary is a gift to the child's nervous system.[1]

If you cannot control the other adult, you can still control the lane you bring. Your lane can be calm, brief, and child-centered: "Hey, sweetheart. I'm glad to see you. Let's grab your bag." Then later, process adult matters with adults.

4) Repair Fast, Repair Small

You will not be regulated all the time. Neither will I. The question is not whether you will miss it. The question is whether you will repair it.

Repair is one of the most stabilizing things a child can witness: an adult owning their tone, making it right, and restoring connection. Co-regulation guidance emphasizes calm, consistent support and coaching; repair is a form of coaching because it teaches the child what to do when they mess up.4

Two-sentence repair (to a child): "I got too sharp. That was not your fault. I'm sorry. You are safe with me."

Two-sentence repair (to a co-parent, when needed): "My tone was not helpful. I'm resetting. Let's keep this child-focused and logistical."

When Adults Fight, Children's Bodies Pay

One reason I am so direct when adults expose children to conflict is because the research is clear: children's stress systems respond to what happens between the adults. Studies have linked children's distress responses to interparental conflict with elevated cortisol reactivity.6 Even when adults believe kids are "fine," children's bodies are often telling the truth first.

This doesn't mean every disagreement is damaging. It means chronic, intense, unresolved conflict becomes an environment. And kid-first co-parenting refuses to let conflict be the climate.

For the One Who Picks Up the Pieces
If you are the stable adult in a chaotic system, you may be carrying grief, resentment, and exhaustion. You might look at an absent or unwell parent and feel anger rise: "Why do I have to do this alone?" That anger is understandable. It often hides a deeper sorrow: "This is not how it was supposed to be."

But here is a kid-first truth: bitterness is an adult emotion, and it belongs in adult spaces. Children should not be recruited to hold it. They can know reality without being trained to despise a parent.

Honoring an unwell or absent parent does not mean pretending. It means speaking with dignity while telling the truth. It also means teaching the child to receive whatever healthy connection is possible without carrying your anger like a backpack.

A simple reframing can help: instead of "Your parent never shows up," try, "I'm glad you got time with them today." Instead of "They don't care," try, "Adults sometimes have struggles that make consistency hard. Our job is to keep you safe and loved." This protects the child's belonging while keeping reality intact.

And for you, the one carrying so much: get care. Co-regulation only works when the caregiver has enough internal regulation to offer. The practice brief on co-regulation explicitly notes that caregivers will only be effective at co-regulation if they can successfully self-regulate.4 Sometimes the most kid-first thing you can do is to build your own support system so your child is not your only source of comfort.

Closing Prayer
God, steady my spirit when conflict rises.

Help me notice the age of my wound without letting it drive the car.

Give me courage to pause, humility to repair, and strength to choose peace over power.

Protect these children from carrying what the adults have not resolved. Let my calm be a shelter, and let Your presence be our safety. Amen.

In the next chapter: we'll focus on two stories, one home—and keep translating kid-first values into daily, doable steps.

Kid-First takeaway: calm is contagious. Your regulated presence teaches your child's brain what safety feels like.

Chapter 2 Endnotes (APA 7th Edition)

1. Porges, S. W. (2022). Polyvagal theory: A science of safety. Frontiers in Integrative Neuroscience, 16, 871227. https://doi.org/10.3389/fnint.2022.871227

2. Arnsten, A. F. T., Raskind, M. A., Taylor, F. B., & Connor, D. F. (2015). The effects of stress exposure on prefrontal cortex: Translating basic research into successful treatments for post-traumatic stress disorder. Neurobiology of Stress, 1, 89–99. https://doi.org/10.1016/j.ynstr.2014.10.002

3. Arnsten, A. F. T. (2015). Stress weakens prefrontal networks: Molecular insults to higher cognition. Nature Neuroscience, 18, 1376–1385. https://doi.org/10.1038/nn.4087

4. Rosanbalm, K. D., & Murray, D. W. (2017). Caregiver co-regulation across development: A practice brief (OPRE Brief #2017-80). Office of Planning, Research and Evaluation, Administration for Children and Families, U.S. Department of Health and Human Services.

5. Bornstein, M. H., & Esposito, G. (2023). Coregulation: A multilevel approach via biology

and behavior. Children, 10(8), 1323.
https://doi.org/10.3390/children10081323

6. Davies, P. T., Sturge-Apple, M. L., Cicchetti, D.,
& Cummings, E. M. (2008). Adrenocortical
underpinnings of children's psychological
reactivity to interparental conflict. Child
Development, 79(6), 1693–1706.
https://doi.org/10.1111/j.1467-8624.2008.01219.x

7. van der Kolk, B. A. (2014). The body keeps the
score: Brain, mind, and body in the healing of
trauma. Viking.

Chapter 3
Two Stories, One Home

How to stop fighting the surface and start protecting the child

The conflict is rarely about what it looks like

Most co-parenting conflict happens on the surface: bedtime, pickup time, screen limits, homework, who buys the shoes, who forgot the inhaler, who is "too strict," who is "too soft."

But underneath the surface, something else is usually driving the storm.

Two adults can look at the same child and see two different stories. Two adults can live in the same family system and carry two different sets of invisible rules: what respect looks like, what safety means, what "good parenting" requires, what a child should be able to handle, what should never be said out loud.

When those invisible rules collide, it can feel personal. It can feel like, "You're not listening to me," or "You don't care," or "You always do this."

Kid-first co-parenting asks a different question: "What is the child experiencing while we argue about our stories?"

Because children don't only experience what we decide. They experience how we decide.

Two stories: the facts and the meaning we attach
Here is the simplest way to understand most co-parenting tension: there are facts, and there is meaning.

Facts are what happened: the child came home late; the backpack was missing; the parent didn't confirm the schedule; the teacher emailed again.

Meaning is what we tell ourselves about what happened: "They're disrespecting me." "They don't take this seriously." "I'm the only one who cares." "My child is going to end up hurt."

Meaning is powerful because it is often connected to our own history. A small moment can touch a deep fear: abandonment, helplessness, being unseen, losing control, failing our child.

That's why two good people can argue fiercely about something that looks small. They are not fighting about the pickup time. They are fighting about what the pickup time represents.

This is where the kid-first pause becomes more than a technique. It becomes maturity: "What is true right now—and what story am I attaching to it?"

Why this matters so much to children

Children are meaning-makers. They watch adult tone, timing, eye contact, and tension, and they draw conclusions long before they can explain them.

When adult conflict becomes chronic or unpredictable, children often adapt by scanning the room instead of living in it. They become little peacekeepers. They edit their needs. They carry loyalty pressure they never asked for.

Decades of research show that interparental conflict is linked with greater child adjustment difficulties and stronger stress responses, especially when conflict is hostile, unresolved, or pulls children into the middle.[4]

One helpful way to name what children need is emotional security: a child's sense that the family system is steady enough for them to relax, grow, and be a child.[3]

When conflict is sharp or ongoing, it doesn't just make kids sad—it can shake their felt sense of safety. Their body learns to stay on alert.

And conflict doesn't stay neatly in one relationship. Stress between adults often spills over into parenting—shorter patience, harsher tone, less emotional availability.[2]

This is why kid-first co-parenting is not mainly about agreeing on every detail. It is about building enough steadiness that a child is not forced to live braced for the next emotional wave.

Co-Parenting is its own relationship

One of the most freeing truths for many caregivers is this: even if your romantic relationship is broken, your co-parenting relationship still exists.

Coparenting is the way adults support (or undermine) each other in the work of raising a child. It includes how you communicate, how you share responsibility, how you handle disagreements, and whether you protect the child from adult tension.

Research on coparenting describes several overlapping domains that shape child and parent outcomes: how much adults agree on childrearing, how much they support or undermine one another, how labor is divided, and how well they manage family dynamics when stress rises.1

You do not have to like each other to build a functional coparenting relationship. But you do need a shared commitment: the child will not be the place we dump what we can't resolve.

A tool: the Shared Storyline Agreement

When two adults are operating from two different stories, the first goal is not perfect agreement. The goal is a shared storyline the child can live inside.

Think of it as a short covenant—four sentences you can return to when tension rises.

Write it down. Put it in your notes app. Read it before you respond.

The Shared Storyline (four sentences):

- We are building a stable, loving environment where our child can thrive.

- We will not use our child to carry messages, manage emotions, or choose sides.

- We will handle conflict away from the child and return to calm communication as soon as possible.

- When we disagree, we will choose the option that increases safety and predictability for the child.

If you are in a parallel or protective lane, you can still hold this storyline. You may not be able to say it together, but you can live it on your side of the street.

Kitchen-table questions that lower the temperature

When you do have access to conversation (even briefly), try questions that aim for clarity rather than control.

These questions work because they move you from accusation to alignment.

- What does our child need to feel safe this week?

- Where is the conflict exposure highest right now (transitions, texting, bedtime, school issues)?

- What one routine can we keep consistent across homes—even if everything else differs?

- What is one thing you do that helps our child, that I can affirm honestly?

- What boundary would reduce chaos immediately?

Notice what these questions do: they don't require you to agree on everything. They require you to agree on what protects the child.

Simple scripts (when stories collide)

When you feel misunderstood: "I think we're attaching different meanings to the same moment. Can we name the facts first?"

When you need to de-escalate: "I want to keep this calm for the child. I'm going to pause and come back."

When you need a boundary: "I'm not discussing this in front of the child. We can talk by text/email later."

When you want to affirm without pretending: "I can appreciate the good you bring to our child, even when this is hard."

When you're in parallel parenting: "I'll keep communication brief and focused on logistics. Please confirm plans by ___."

A Small Step This Week
This week, don't try to fix the whole system. Choose one place where your child feels the most "caught" and protect it.

Pick one:

• A no-conflict zone around transitions (no arguing at the door, no sharp handoffs, no emotional speeches).

• A no-messenger rule (no messages through the child, ever).

• A shared storyline statement you read before you respond to triggers.

Stability is built the same way faith is built: one faithful choice at a time.

Closing prayer
God, give me wisdom to see what is really happening beneath the surface.

When my fear gets loud, help me return to truth and steadiness.

Teach me to protect this child from carrying adult weight—spoken or unspoken.

Help me choose words that build safety, and boundaries that build peace.

Next: we'll focus on the capacity gap—and keep translating kid-first values into daily, doable steps.

And when I don't get it right, give me humility to repair quickly and love steadily.

Amen.

Kid-First takeaway: the win is a child who feels loved, safe, and protected—while adult problems stay in adult hands.

Chapter 3 Endnotes (APA 7th Edition)
1. Feinberg, M. E. (2003). The internal structure and ecological context of coparenting: A framework for research and intervention.

Parenting: Science and Practice, 3(2), 95–131.
https://doi.org/10.1207/S15327922PAR0302_01

2. Erel, O., & Burman, B. (1995). Interrelatedness
of marital relations and parent–child relations: A
meta-analytic review. Psychological Bulletin,
118(1), 108–132.

3. Davies, P. T., Harold, G. T., Goeke-Morey, M.
C., & Cummings, E. M. (2002). Child emotional
security and interparental conflict. Monographs of
the Society for Research in Child Development,
67(3, Serial No. 270), 1–115.

4. van Eldik, W. M., Luijk, M. P. C. M., Parry, L.
Q., & Prinzie, P. (2020). The interparental
relationship: Meta-analytic associations with
children's maladjustment and responses to
interparental conflict. Psychological Bulletin,
146(7), 553–594.
https://doi.org/10.1037/bul0000233

Chapter 4
The Capacity Gap

When adults don't have the same ability to show up

Capacity is not character

Some families are not dealing with a simple difference in parenting style. They are dealing with a capacity gap.

One adult can show up consistently—emotionally, practically, financially, and relationally. Another adult shows up in waves, disappears for seasons, or becomes unpredictable under stress. Sometimes it's illness. Sometimes it's addiction. Sometimes it's immaturity. Sometimes it's a nervous system that has never learned steadiness. Sometimes it's simply the weight of life and the absence of support.

Whatever the reason, the child experiences the same outcome: inconsistency.

Kid-first co-parenting refuses to turn that inconsistency into a character assassination campaign. It also refuses to pretend it isn't happening.

Here is the line we will walk throughout this chapter: We can honor a parent's dignity and still build the child's stability.

Why capacity gaps shake children

When adults have uneven capacity, children often live in a chronic state of uncertainty: Who is picking me up? Who is coming? Who is safe today? What mood will be waiting on the other side of the door?

That uncertainty isn't "just inconvenient." It's stressful. And stress shapes behavior, attention, sleep, learning, and emotional regulation.

A 2024 systematic review with meta-analysis found that parental stress is associated with children's emotional and behavioral problems—meaning what burdens the adult nervous system often shows up in the child's nervous system, too.[1]

This is why capacity work is kid-first work. If we can lower chaos and increase predictability, we aren't just making life easier—we are protecting a child's development.

The kid-first reframe: coverage beats fairness

When capacity is uneven, many caregivers get stuck in one of two exhausting questions:

• "Why do I have to do everything?"

- "Why can't they just show up like I do?"

Those questions make sense. They are honest. They are also a dead end if we try to solve them inside the child's world.

Kid-first asks a different question: "What level of coverage does this child need—and who can actually provide it?"

Fairness is about equal contribution. Coverage is about steady care.

In a capacity gap, you may never get equal. But you can build steady.

The battery is real (and exhaustion has consequences)

Many adults are not starting the day at 100%. Some are starting at 30%. Some are starting in survival mode. And when parenting demands outrun resources for too long, the result can be parental burnout—an exhaustion-and-detachment pattern that grows from a chronic imbalance of risks over supports.2

This matters because exhaustion is not neutral. In a longitudinal study, parental burnout symptoms—beginning with exhaustion—were linked over time to emotional distancing and "feeling fed up," which in turn predicted increases in parental violence.3

Let's say this clearly and compassionately: when an adult is depleted and unregulated, the child is at greater risk. So the kid-first goal is not to shame exhausted adults. It is to build enough support, boundaries, and structure that exhaustion does not become danger.

A tool: the Capacity Map
Before you can build a stable plan, you need a clear picture of what is actually true—not what you wish were true, not what someone promises in a good mood, but what is consistent over time.

Use this tool to assess each caregiver's current capacity in key areas. For each domain, mark Strong, Limited, or Variable, then write one sentence of evidence (what you've consistently observed over time). Finally, decide who owns that domain—and what the backup plan is.

Rating Key

• Strong: reliable and steady most of the time

• Limited: consistently weak or unavailable in this area

• Variable: inconsistent; depends on mood, stress, season, or support

Step 1: Rate Each Domain
(Repeat for each caregiver)

Caregiver Name: _____

Role (parent / grandparent / etc.):

_____

1) Safety & Supervision

☐ Strong ☐ Limited ☐ Variable

Evidence (what makes you say this?):

_____

Owner for this domain: _____

Backup/Village: _____

2) Daily Logistics (school, pickups, routines)

☐ Strong ☐ Limited ☐ Variable

Evidence:

_____

_____

Owner: _____

Backup/Village: _____

3) Emotional Steadiness (tone, repair, calm)

☐ Strong ☐ Limited ☐ Variable

Evidence:

_____

_____

Owner: _____

Backup/Village: _____

4) Communication (conflict management, follow-through)

☐ Strong ☐ Limited ☐ Variable

Evidence:

_____

_____

Owner: _____

Backup/Village: _____

5) Medical & School Responsibilities (appointments, meds, forms, teacher contact)

☐ Strong ☐ Limited ☐ Variable

Evidence:

_____

_____

Owner: _____

Backup/Village: _____

6) Financial / Material Provision (basic needs, supplies, consistency)

☐ Strong   ☐ Limited   ☐ Variable

Evidence:

_____

_____

Owner: _____

Backup/Village: _____

Step 2: Decide "Who Owns What" (One Line Summary)

• Primary Stability Lead for this season:

_____

_____

• Domains owned by Caregiver A:

_____

_____

• Domains owned by Caregiver B:

_____

_____

• Village / Backup supports (names + contact):

_____

_____

Step 3: Build One Minimum Safety Rule (Non-Negotiable)

Our non-negotiable safety baseline is:

_____

_____

_____

(Example: "No conflict in front of the child." "No impaired driving." "Meds stay consistent.")

Important note: This is not a scorecard to shame someone. It's a clarity tool to protect a child. The child doesn't need you to pretend. The child needs you to plan.

This is not a scorecard to shame someone. It's a clarity tool to protect a child. The child doesn't need you to pretend. The child needs you to plan.

Build a Minimum Viable Parenting Plan

When capacity is uneven, you don't start by negotiating every preference. You start by building a minimum viable plan: the smallest set of agreements that creates a stable week.

Minimum viable means five anchors:

- A predictable schedule (and a backup plan for when someone can't follow through).

- One communication channel (text/email/app) that stays logistical and child-centered.

- Two or three non-negotiables that protect the child (safety rules, no adult conflict in front of the child, no using the child as a messenger).

- Transition rules (handoffs stay brief, calm, and child-focused).

- A support list (one counselor/pastor/mentor, one family ally, one emergency contact).

If you can get these five anchors in place, you have already reduced the child's stress load—even if the broader family system is still messy.

Honor without enabling

Honoring an adult with limited capacity does not mean covering harm or pretending instability is normal. It means you speak with dignity while you tell the truth and set boundaries.

Kids do not benefit from being trained to hate a parent. They also do not benefit from being trained to ignore reality. The healthiest middle is this: we name the child's lived experience, and we keep adult judgments in adult spaces.

Here are kid-first scripts you can actually use:

To the other caregiver (clear + calm): "I'm going to build stability for the child. Here is the plan I'm following. If you can participate, I welcome it. If you can't right now, we will keep the child covered."

When promises don't match reality: "I'm going to make decisions based on what is consistent, not what is promised. For the child's sake, we need predictability."

To a child (age-appropriate, no diagnosis): "Sometimes adults have a hard time being consistent. That is not your fault. Our job is to keep you safe and cared for."

To yourself (when bitterness rises): "My anger is real. I will process it with adults, not in front of the child."

For the ones who pick up the pieces
If you are the one doing most of the work, you may carry anger that feels like it lives in your bones. That anger is often grief in disguise: grief that your child's story is harder than it should be; grief that you are alone in the weight; grief that someone else gets to opt out while you stay responsible.

Kid-first co-parenting does not require you to pretend that grief doesn't exist. It requires that you relocate it to the right place.

Adult grief belongs with adult support—pastors, counselors, mentors, trusted friends—so the child does not become the emotional container for your pain.

Here is a practical reset: instead of rehearsing what the other adult should be doing, name what the child needs today. Then do the next right thing with steady love.

A bitterness-to-stability practice (3 steps):

1. Name the cost (to yourself, privately): "This is heavy. I'm tired."

2. Name the boundary (out loud, calmly): "I won't argue in front of the child. I'll respond later."

3. Name the blessing (to the child): "I love you. You're safe. I've got you."

When the whole system lacks capacity
Sometimes the question isn't, "Which parent has more capacity?" Sometimes the question is, "Where is the safe adult?"

If no adult in the immediate system can reliably provide safety and stability, kid-first wisdom expands the circle. This is where the village is not optional—it's protective.

In those seasons, your next step is usually one of these:

- Pull in consistent supports (trusted family, church leadership, a therapist, a pediatrician, a school counselor).

- Create a written safety-and-coverage plan (who supervises, who transports, who is the emergency contact).

- If safety is at risk—physical harm, credible threats, unsafe supervision—seek immediate professional help through the appropriate channels in your region.

This book cannot replace professional or legal guidance, but it can help you name the principle: stability is the priority, and safety is the baseline.

A Small Step This Week
This week, choose one stabilizing decision that is not dependent on another adult's mood.

Pick one:

- A consistent morning or bedtime routine (same order, same tone, same ending).

- A calm, brief transition rule (no conflict at the door; no emotional speeches; child-centered handoff).

- A communication boundary (one channel; no rapid-fire texting; 24-hour pause when possible).

- One support call (pastor, counselor, mentor) to process your grief outside of the child's hearing.

Chapter 4 Endnotes (APA 7th Edition)

1. Ribas, L. H., Montezano, B. B., Nieves, M., Kampmann, L. B., & Jansen, K. (2024). The role of parental stress on emotional and behavioral problems in offspring: A systematic review with meta-analysis. Jornal de Pediatria, 100(6), 565–585. https://doi.org/10.1016/j.jped.2024.02.003

2. Mikolajczak, M., & Roskam, I. (2018). A theoretical and clinical framework for parental burnout: The balance between risks and resources (BR2). Frontiers in Psychology, 9, 886. https://doi.org/10.3389/fpsyg.2018.00886

3. Schittek, A., Roskam, I., & Mikolajczak, M. (2024). Parental burnout stages and their link to parental violence: A longitudinal study. Journal of Applied Developmental Psychology, 95, 101717. https://doi.org/10.1016/j.appdev.2024.101717

In the pages ahead, we'll focus on when no one has capacity—and keep translating kid-first values into daily, doable steps.

If you are the one picking up the pieces, you may also be grieving. Not just the workload—but the loss of what you hoped your child would have: steadier adults, fewer transitions, a simpler story. Grief does not mean you are weak or bitter. It means you are human. Name the loss in an adult place, get support, and then return to the child's needs with steadiness.

Closing prayer

God, give me wisdom for the reality I'm in—not the reality I wish I had.

Help me honor people with dignity while also telling the truth and setting boundaries that protect this child.

When I feel bitter, meet me in my grief and give me adult support so my child does not carry adult weight.

Give me courage to build stability—steady, practical, faithful stability—one day at a time.

Amen.

Kid-First takeaway: plan for reality, not ideals. Capacity can change, but children need steadiness today.

Chapter 5
When Caregivers Lack Capacity

If Your Capacity Is Low Right Now

This section is for the parent who wants to show up well but feels flooded, exhausted, impulsive, or emotionally raw. Low capacity does not mean you don't love your child. It means your nervous system bandwidth is low. In these seasons, your job is not to negotiate co-parenting dynamics or win arguments—it is to protect your child's safety and stability by choosing a simpler plan.

Think of it like first aid. When you're bleeding, you don't start training for a marathon. You stop the bleeding. You ask for help. You stabilize. Then, as strength returns, you can build more.

A Low-Capacity Quick Plan (4 steps)

- Safety first: If you are dysregulated, sleep-deprived, using substances, or feel out of control, do not try to "push through" solo parenting. Call a safe adult and choose supervision or backup care. Kid-first does not require heroics—only honesty.

- Stability over intensity: Choose the simplest plan you can keep. Predictable routines (meals, bedtime, school pickup) matter more than big emotional conversations.

- One-lane communication: Keep messages brief and logistical. Don't process feelings by text. If a conversation escalates, pause and return later when regulated.

- Repair, then return: If you snapped, shut down, or spiraled, repair quickly and gently. A short apology and reconnection protects your child from carrying shame or fear.

Two scripts (use them—don't over-explain)
To another caregiver/helper: "I'm not at my best today. For the child's stability, I need backup care. Can you cover from ___ to ___? I'll confirm the plan by ___. Thank you."

To the child (age-appropriate): "I'm having a hard moment, and it's not your fault. I'm going to take a pause and get help so you stay safe and cared for. I love you, and I'll be back with you soon."

A word about treatment and support
If your capacity is low often, the most loving kid-first step may be building a consistent support plan: treatment, sleep protection, medication management if prescribed, and a small village who knows what to do when you're struggling. This is

not punishment. It is stewardship. Children relax when adults are honest and supported.

Building a Circle of Care so a child is never the safety plan

When the system is shaky, the child gets shaky

Some chapters in this book assume at least one adult in the system can show up consistently—maybe not perfectly, but steadily.

This chapter is for the families where that assumption doesn't hold.

There are situations where multiple adults are struggling at once: one adult is inconsistent, another is overwhelmed, another is reactive, another is exhausted, and the "village" is in conflict with itself. Sometimes the child is bouncing between homes. Sometimes the child is in one home, but the adults in that home are not unified.

In these stories, adults often ask a painful question: Where does the kid go?

Kid-first answers with a principle before it offers a plan:

A child should never be the safety plan.

A child should never be the emotional stabilizer.

A child should never be the messenger, the referee, the therapist, the peacekeeper, or the reason an adult holds it together.

When adults don't have capacity, kid-first care expands the circle. We build a structure that holds the child even when the adults wobble.

A clarification: "village" is not a crowd
When people hear "it takes a village," they sometimes picture a crowd of opinions, a revolving door of helpers, and a child pulled in ten different directions.

That is not a village. That is noise.

A kid-first village is smaller and steadier. It is a Circle of Care: a defined set of adults who agree on stability, protect the child from adult conflict, and communicate clearly.

Kinship care—when relatives or trusted family-like adults step in—is one common form of a circle of care. It can be informal or formal, temporary or long-term, but the purpose is the same: to keep the child connected and covered.

Child welfare guidance describes kinship care as relatives and "fictive kin" stepping in to care for children when parents are unable to do so.[1]

Research syntheses have found that, when children cannot remain safely with parents, placement with kin is often associated with benefits such as greater stability and better well-being outcomes compared to non-kin foster care—while also acknowledging the real hardships kin caregivers face.24

Pediatric guidance likewise emphasizes that kinship families often carry both strengths and vulnerabilities, and they need practical support—not assumptions that they can absorb new responsibilities without help.3

The kid-first goal: one safe adult, one steady plan
In high-chaos systems, adults often try to solve everything at once: relationships, history, apologies, court, finances, parenting styles, who hurt whom, who is to blame.

Kid-first starts smaller. It asks: What does this child need to feel safe this week?

In most unstable systems, the answer is surprisingly consistent:

• One safe adult who is predictably available.

• One plan that does not change daily based on moods.

• One communication structure that reduces conflict exposure.

• One backup layer so the child is not dropped when adults collapse.

This is not about creating a perfect family. It is about creating a breathable environment.

The Circle of Care Framework (three rings)
Picture three rings around the child. Not three groups to argue with—three layers of protection.

Ring 1: The Steady Care Team

These are the adults who provide primary routines and decision-making. They are the child's "yes" adults: yes to safety, yes to predictability, yes to school, yes to bedtime, yes to medical care.

Ring 2: The Practical Support Team

These adults help the Steady Care Team stay steady: transportation backup, meals, respite, homework help, childcare coverage.

Ring 3: The Professional Team

These are the helpers with training and authority: pediatrician, therapist, school counselor, caseworker, attorney, parenting coordinator, pastor (when appropriate), and other community supports.

The child does not manage these rings. Adults do.

A Circle of Care works best when roles are written down.

Circle of Care – Write It Down

Ring 1: Steady Care Team (primary routines and decisions)

Names:

_____

_____

Role(s) they own (circle or list): safety / supervision • daily routines • school • medical

Contact info:

_____

_____

Notes:

_____

_____

_____

Ring 2: Practical Support Team (backup helpers who keep the system steady)

Name #1: _____

Phone/Email: _____

What they can cover: rides / meals / respite / childcare / homework / other:

_____

Name #2: _____

Phone/Email: _____

What they can cover: rides / meals / respite / childcare / homework / other:

_____

Name #3: _____

Phone/Email: _____

What they can cover: rides / meals / respite / childcare / homework / other:

_____

Ring 3: Professional Team (trained supports who add structure and protection)

Pediatrician: _____

Phone: _____

Therapist/Counselor: _____

Phone: _____

School counselor/point person: _____

Phone/Email: _____

Attorney / parenting coordinator / caseworker (if applicable):

_____

Pastor / ministry support (if appropriate):

_____

_____

Other community supports:

_____

_____

Contact / Notes:

_____

_____

Closing note: This table is not bureaucracy. It is mercy. It keeps the child from being the one who has to wonder, "Who will show up for me today?"

A tool: the Circle of Care Agreement

Most chaotic systems don't collapse because people don't care. They collapse because nobody agrees on who is responsible for what.

So the Circle of Care begins with a short agreement. If you are working with a therapist or pastor, this can be built in session. If you are navigating a high-conflict situation, a written agreement can also be supported by structured professionals such as parenting coordination, when appropriate.

Parenting coordination is one structured model used in high-conflict family systems to reduce child exposure to conflict and increase clarity and compliance with child-focused plans.5

Circle of Care Agreement (keep it simple):

- We will not argue in front of the child or during transitions.

- We will not use the child to carry messages, manage emotions, or report on other adults.

- We will speak about all caregivers with basic dignity in front of the child (truthful, not flattering; respectful, not resentful).

- We will follow one written schedule. Changes must be confirmed by ___. If not confirmed, the schedule stands.

- We will keep communication brief and logistical. When emotions rise, we pause before responding.

- We will name safety concerns to the appropriate adults and professionals—never to the child.

- When we don't agree, we will choose the decision that increases safety and predictability for the child.

If someone cannot honor this agreement, they are not "bad." They may be unwell, overwhelmed, or immature. But kid-first reality is this: the child still needs the agreement to be lived by the adults who can.

Telling the truth without training contempt
In unstable systems, children often feel two things at once: love for an adult, and disappointment in that adult's inconsistency.

Our job is not to erase either feeling. Our job is to keep the child from being shaped by bitterness.

Children become more stable when they are allowed to receive whatever good is available—

without being asked to deny the hard parts or to carry adult judgment.

This is not about forcing gratitude for crumbs. It is about protecting a child's attachment world from adult contempt.

Here is a kid-first sentence to keep near your heart: We can honor an adult's dignity without asking a child to live inside the adult's instability.

Kid-first scripts (no diagnosis, just reality):

To a child (after a letdown): "I'm sorry. I know you were looking forward to that. This is not your fault. We have a plan, and you're safe."

To a child (when time does happen): "I'm glad you got that time. It's okay to enjoy it. If you feel mixed up later, you can tell me."

To a caregiver who is angry: "Your feelings are real. Let's process them with adults, not in front of the child."

To extended family: "We can talk privately about concerns. In front of the child, we keep it calm and respectful."

Rapid stabilization: what to do in the next 72 hours

When a family system is actively unstable, you do not need a perfect long-term plan first. You need a short-term stabilizing plan that protects the next few days.

Here are the priorities, in order:

- Safety baseline: who is safe for supervision today? (Not who is "supposed" to be safe—who is actually safe.)

- Coverage: who does pickups, meals, bedtime, and school communication for the next 72 hours?

- Conflict reduction: choose one channel for adult communication and keep it logistical.

- Transition rule: handoffs are brief, calm, and child-centered; no arguing at the door.

- One wise voice: involve one steady professional or leader (therapist, pediatrician, school counselor, pastor) to help hold the plan.

If you do these five things, you have already lowered the child's stress load—before you solve the deeper story.

When the village is fighting

One of the hardest realities in kinship and village systems is this: the helpers can become another source of conflict.

Grandparents argue with parents. Aunts and uncles take sides. Church friends offer advice that becomes pressure. The child becomes the center of a tug-of-war.

Kid-first care requires a boundary here: adults can disagree, but the child will not be the battlefield.

If your village is fighting, narrow the circle. Stability is not built by the loudest voices. It is built by the steadiest ones.

A narrowing question that helps:

"Who consistently chooses the child's peace over adult power?"

A Small Step This Week

This week, build your Circle of Care on paper— even if the system is messy.

Do three things:

- Write down Ring 1, Ring 2, and Ring 3 names and phone numbers.

- Write one simple schedule for the next seven days with a backup plan.

- Choose one sentence you will use to protect the child from adult conflict: "We can talk about that later. Right now we're keeping this calm for the child."

Your child does not need you to be heroic. Your child needs you to be steady.

Closing prayer
God, when the adults around this child are strained, help me become steady.

Give me wisdom to build a plan that holds—especially when emotions rise.

What we'll tackle next: we'll focus on communication that protects the child—and keep translating kid-first values into daily, doable steps.

Help me honor people with dignity while also telling the truth and setting boundaries that protect what is sacred.

Surround this child with safe love. Expand the circle. Quiet the chaos. Strengthen the helpers.

And let this child grow up breathing peace, even in an imperfect story.

Amen.

Kid-First takeaway: plan for reality, not ideals. Capacity can change, but children need steadiness today.

Chapter 5 Endnotes (APA 7th Edition)

1. Child Welfare Information Gateway. (n.d.). Kinship care. U.S. Department of Health and Human Services, Administration for Children and Families, Children's Bureau. https://www.childwelfare.gov/topics/permanency/kinship-care/

2. Winokur, M., Holtan, A., & Batchelder, K. E. (2018). Systematic review of kinship care effects on safety, permanency, and well-being outcomes. Research on Social Work Practice, 28(1), 19–32. https://doi.org/10.1177/1049731515620843

3. Rubin, D., Springer, S. H., Zlotnik, S., Kang-Yi, C. D., & Council on Foster Care, Adoption, and Kinship Care. (2017). Needs of kinship care families and pediatric practice. Pediatrics, 139(4), e20170099. https://doi.org/10.1542/peds.2017-0099

4. Cochrane. (n.d.). Kinship care for the safety, permanency, and well-being of children removed from the home for maltreatment. https://www.cochrane.org/evidence/CD006546_kinship-care-safety-permanency-and-well-being-maltreated-children

5. Association of Family and Conciliation Courts. (2019). Guidelines for parenting coordination. https://www.afccnet.org/Portals/0/Committees/Guidelines%20for%20Parenting%20Coordination%202019.pdf

Chapter 6
Communication That Protects the Child

How to talk (and text) without handing your stress to your kids

The child feels the way adults communicate
Families often assume that as long as children don't hear the whole argument, they're protected.

But children are excellent at reading what is unspoken. They pick up tone. They sense tension in the car. They hear the pause before a parent answers. They watch faces after a phone call. They notice when adults slam cabinets or go silent.

So kid-first co-parenting is not only about what you say. It's about what your child experiences while you are saying it.

This chapter is about a simple goal: communication that lowers conflict exposure for the child.

Research on co-parenting programs suggests that structured skill-building—psychoeducation, communication tools, and practice—can improve co-parenting quality and parent well-being, even across diverse family situations.1

In other words: you don't have to "feel close" to communicate well. You can learn a better way.

Choose the lane before you choose the words
Before we talk about what to say, we choose the lane you're in right now.

Cordial lane: you can discuss, problem-solve, and collaborate without escalation.

Parallel lane: communication is limited and structured; you coordinate logistics and protect the child from conflict exposure.

Protective lane: safety is at risk; boundaries are tighter and support is higher.

Your lane determines your communication expectations. The biggest mistake families make is trying to communicate like cordial co-parents when the relationship is actually parallel or protective.

If you choose the right lane, you stop setting yourself up for repeated emotional collisions.

Two kid-first communication rules
Rule one: Keep it child-centered and specific.

Rule two: Keep it calm and brief.

When communication becomes a trial—long explanations, past grievances, sarcasm, "you always," "you never"—it stops being about the child and starts being about power and pain.

You may be completely right about what happened. But if the child pays the price through escalating conflict, the cost is too high.

A tool that works in real life: BIFF
When communication is strained, written messages often become the battlefield. Texts turn into arguments. Emails turn into emotional dumping. Social media becomes a stage.

One practical framework that many family-court and clinical professionals recommend for high-conflict written communication is BIFF: Brief, Informative, Friendly, and Firm.2

Here is what BIFF looks like:

- Brief: One topic. One request. One clear line. (Not a paragraph about history.)

- Informative: Facts and logistics, not character judgments.

- Friendly: Neutral warmth, not sarcasm. (Professional tone.)

- Firm: Clear boundary, clear next step, no debate invitation.

BIFF example (parallel lane):

"Confirming pickup: I'll be there at 5:30 p.m. at the usual spot. If you need to change the time, please let me know by 3:00."

Notice what is not included: accusations, explanations, old wounds, and emotional bait.

The Alignment Meeting (30 minutes, not a therapy session)

If you are in the cordial lane—or if you are trying to build a healthier parallel lane—schedule a short, structured meeting.

This is not the meeting where you solve your relationship history. It is the meeting where you protect the child's week.

Set a timer for 30 minutes. End on time. If you cannot stay calm, move back to parallel lane communication and get support.

Use this agenda:

- Start with the shared goal: "We're here to build stability for the child."

- Name the non-negotiables (2–3 only): safety rules, no conflict in front of the child, no child as messenger.

- Agree on one routine that stays consistent across homes (bedtime order, homework window, morning rhythm).

- Confirm logistics for the next 7–14 days (schedule, school needs, appointments).

- Choose the communication structure (one channel; response windows; what counts as urgent).

- End with one sentence of mutual dignity: "Thank you for working toward stability."

If you have never seen a calm, structured meeting modeled, this may feel awkward. That's okay. Structure is what keeps the meeting from becoming emotional warfare.

Repair is a child's oxygen
Even in the best families, adults miss it sometimes. Tone gets sharp. Stress leaks. Words land wrong.

Kid-first families do not pretend they never mess up. They repair quickly.

Repair teaches a child: conflict is survivable, relationships can be safe again, and I am not responsible for managing adult emotions.

A simple repair script is enough:

"I'm sorry. I was frustrated and I spoke too sharply. That wasn't your responsibility. I'm going to calm down and try again."

When communication is impossible

Some readers will say, "This sounds nice, but we cannot have meetings. We cannot talk without escalation."

That is real. In those cases, kid-first care becomes structured communication plus outside support.

Family-court and mental-health guidelines describe parenting coordination as one structured approach used in some high-conflict contexts to reduce child exposure to conflict and support compliance with child-focused plans.

When it is appropriate and available, structured professional support can help families move from chaos to clarity.3

This book cannot tell you what your court system requires, but it can remind you of the principle: the child deserves a plan that does not depend on adult mood.

A Small Step This Week

This week, choose one communication change that lowers conflict exposure immediately.

Pick one:

- Switch to one written channel for logistics (text/email/app) and keep it BIFF.

- Adopt a 24-hour pause rule for non-urgent issues.

- Create a "no conflict at transitions" boundary and rehearse the script: "We can talk later. Keeping this calm for the child."

- Schedule a 30-minute Alignment Meeting (if cordial lane is possible).

- Choose one adult support person to help you process anger outside of the child's hearing.

Small communication shifts can change the emotional climate faster than you think—because children breathe the climate you create.

Closing prayer

God, put a guard over my mouth and a guard over my phone.

When I feel triggered, help me pause before I spill my stress into this child's world.

Give me words that are true and kind, boundaries that are firm and peaceful, and humility to repair quickly when I miss it.

Teach me to be a steady presence—so my child can be a child.

Amen.

Kid-First takeaway: safety is not negotiable. When risk is present, structure and support come before togetherness.

Chapter 6 Endnotes (APA 7th Edition)

1. Nunes, C. E., de Roten, Y., El Ghaziri, N., Favez, N., & Darwiche, J. (2021). Co-parenting programs: A systematic review and meta-analysis. Family Relations, 70(3), 759–776.

2. Eddy, B., Burns, A. T., & Chafin, K. (2020). BIFF for Coparent Communication: Your guide to difficult texts, emails, and social media posts. Unhooked Books/High Conflict Institute Press.

3. Association of Family and Conciliation Courts. (2019). Guidelines for Parenting Coordination. https://www.afccnet.org/Portals/0/Committees/Guidelines%20for%20Parenting%20Coordination%202019.pdf

Chapter 7
House Rules That Hold

How to build predictability across homes without trying to control everything

Why rules matter more in complicated families
When life is simple, kids can absorb a lot of variation. Different bedtimes on weekends. Different routines during sports season. A late dinner here and there.

But when family structure is complicated—two homes, multiple caregivers, uneven capacity—kids need something steadier than adult mood.

They need predictability.

House rules are not about becoming strict. They are about becoming stable.

And stability is one of the most loving things you can give a child.

Research on parenting has long shown that rules land differently depending on the emotional climate they are delivered in—warmth, responsiveness, and consistent structure shape how children interpret and internalize guidance.13

Meta-analytic work also suggests that supportive, structured parenting is associated with fewer internalizing difficulties (like anxiety and depression), while harsh or inconsistent patterns are linked with higher risk.2

Sameness is not the goal. Stability is.
Many co-parents get stuck trying to make both homes identical. That sounds noble, but it often becomes a control war.

Kid-first parenting doesn't require sameness. It requires stability.

Stability means a child can predict what happens next in the areas that matter most.

So instead of trying to agree on everything, choose a small set of rules that hold across homes— especially around safety, respect, and routines that affect school and health.

The four anchors of house rules that hold
Choose 2–3 rules in each pillar. Keep them simple. Post them. Repeat them. Repair when you miss it.

1) Safety

- Seatbelts, car seats, safe supervision, medication rules.

- No unsafe adults around the child.

- Clear rules for internet, devices, and privacy.

2) Respect

- We don't yell at each other.
- We don't hit, threaten, or intimidate.
- We talk to adults with respect, and adults talk to kids with respect.

3) Responsibility

- Homework window or "homework first" routine.
- Basic chores or contribution appropriate to age.
- Restitution when harm is done (clean up, repair, apologize).

4) Rhythm

- A bedtime rhythm (order matters more than the exact time).
- A morning rhythm (wake, dress, breakfast, out the door).
- A transition rhythm (snack, settle, connect, then routine).

A simple alignment method: one page, one month

If you can collaborate, don't try to build a perfect parenting philosophy. Build a one-page plan for the next month.

Write three things:

- Our non-negotiables (5–7 total): safety, respect, and two routines.

- Our logistics (schedule, school needs, medical needs).

- Our communication rules (one channel, response window, BIFF tone).

Then review once a month. Kid-first stability grows through small adjustments, not dramatic overhauls.

When you can't align: build stability on your side of the street

Some readers will say, "The other home will not cooperate."

If that's you, here is your freedom: you can still build house rules that hold in your home.

Children benefit from having at least one predictable environment. Even if the other home is inconsistent, your steadiness becomes a place their nervous system can rest.

In parallel parenting, your goal is not to enforce your rules in the other home. Your goal is to make your home a safe, stable landing pad.

Screens: rhythms, not rigid rules
Screens are one of the most common places adults fight, because screens touch rest, school, behavior, and family connection.

Kid-first wisdom avoids shame-based extremes. It doesn't treat screens like the enemy. It treats disconnection as the enemy.

So instead of only asking, "How do we reduce screen time?" ask, "How do we increase shared time and healthy rhythms?"

A practical tool is a Family Media Plan—agreeing on where screens live, when they rest, what's monitored, and what content is appropriate.

The American Academy of Pediatrics provides resources and a Family Media Plan framework to help families create balanced, intentional screen rhythms.4

Simple kid-first screen rhythms:

- Screens rest during meals and at bedtime.

- Shared viewing when possible (co-view and converse).

- Content is monitored; devices are not private worlds for young children.

- When screens increase, connection also increases (you don't trade relationship for distraction).

Simple scripts

When you're proposing shared rules: "I'm not trying to control your home. I'm trying to give our child predictability. Can we agree on a few non-negotiables?"

When you need to simplify: "Let's keep this small: safety rules, respect rules, and one bedtime rhythm."

When the other home won't align: "I can't control what happens there. I can build steadiness here."

To a child who compares homes: "Different homes can have different rules. In this home, we keep you safe and we treat each other with respect."

A Small Step This Week

This week, choose five rules that will hold in your home no matter what.

Write them on one page. Post them where you can see them.

If you can align with the other home, share them and ask for agreement on the top three.

Then practice the most important parenting skill: consistency with warmth.

In the next chapter: we'll focus on discipline without division—and keep translating kid-first values into daily, doable steps.

Closing prayer

God, help me build a home that feels safe to a child's nervous system.

Give me wisdom to choose rules that guide, not rules that shame.

Help me be consistent without being harsh, and warm without being permissive.

And when our family structure is complicated, let stability be one of the ways love shows up.

Amen.

Kid-First takeaway: the win is a child who feels loved, safe, and protected—while adult problems stay in adult hands.

Chapter 7 Endnotes (APA 7th Edition)

1. Darling, N., & Steinberg, L. (1993). Parenting style as context: An integrative model. Psychological Bulletin, 113(3), 487–496.

2. Pinquart, M. (2017). Associations of parenting dimensions and styles with internalizing symptoms in children and adolescents: A meta-analysis. Marriage & Family Review, 53(7), 613–640.

3. Maccoby, E. E., & Martin, J. A. (1983). Socialization in the context of the family: Parent–child interaction. In P. H. Mussen (Ed.), Handbook of child psychology (Vol. 4, pp. 1–101). Wiley.

4. American Academy of Pediatrics. (n.d.). Media and children communication toolkit / family media plan. https://www.healthychildren.org/English/media/Pages/default.aspx

Chapter 8
Discipline Without Division

Guidance that teaches—without turning your child into the battleground

Discipline is one of the loudest places adults disagree

If you have ever argued about discipline, you are not alone.

Discipline touches everything: respect, safety, faith, identity, family history, and the deep fear that your child will suffer if you don't get it right.

That's why discipline disagreements can feel personal, even when both adults love the child.

But kids don't experience your good intentions. They experience your environment.

So kid-first co-parenting begins with a commitment: we will not make discipline the place our child learns division.

A faithful reframe: discipline is guidance, not pain

Many of us grew up with the idea that discipline had to hurt in order to work. Some of us learned that authority is proved by force, volume, or fear.

But the kid-first goal of discipline is not fear-based control. It is wise, loving guidance that forms character over time.

Discipline is about teaching: what to do instead, how to repair harm, how to regulate emotions, and how to live with boundaries.

The American Academy of Pediatrics emphasizes that effective discipline is rooted in a positive, supportive relationship and that physical punishment and harsh verbal punishment are associated with negative outcomes for children.1

Large-scale meta-analytic research similarly links spanking with increased risk of negative child outcomes, including more aggression and more behavior problems—again reminding us that pain may stop a behavior in the moment, but it does not teach the skills a child needs to grow.2

This chapter is not here to shame your past. It is here to give you a better path forward.

When adults disagree, children feel unsafe—even when nobody is yelling

In two-home or multi-caregiver families, a child is often navigating two different rule systems, two different emotional climates, and two different definitions of "discipline."

Some variation is normal. But when discipline becomes unpredictable—strict one day, permissive the next; calm in one home, harsh in another—children become hypervigilant.

They may act out more, not because they are "bad," but because their nervous system is trying to figure out what works where.

So kid-first discipline asks for one thing first: predictability.

The kid-first discipline triangle: regulate, guide, connect
If you want a simple framework you can remember in the heat of real life, use this triangle:

4. 1) Regulate: Get your nervous system steady before you correct. (A dysregulated adult cannot teach regulation.)

5. 2) Guide: Name what happened and teach what to do next—using consequences that instruct, not shame.

6. 3) Connect: End with relationship. Repair builds trust and makes learning possible.

This mirrors what many child-development thinkers describe as co-regulation: children borrow calm from steady adults before they can generate it on their own.3

It also aligns with decades of work on emotion coaching—helping children name feelings, choose better actions, and repair when harm is done.4

Notice what's missing from the triangle: humiliation. Threats. Fear. Those may create compliance, but they rarely create character.

The Discipline Non-Negotiables (what both homes can usually agree on)
Even when adults have different personalities or styles, most can agree on a few kid-first non-negotiables. These are the anchors that keep discipline from becoming chaos.

Aim for five. Keep them short. Repeat them often.

- We keep bodies safe. (No hitting, no intimidation.)

- We speak with respect. (Adults model the tone they require.)

- We repair harm. (We clean up, make it right, apologize, restore.)

- We don't discipline in anger. (We pause, then return.)

- We don't use the child as a messenger about discipline disagreements.

If you can align on these five, your child will experience more safety—even if the details differ between homes.

Consequences that teach (not consequences that shame)

Kid-first consequences do two things at the same time:

• They stop harm.

• They teach skill and responsibility.

The simplest way to choose a consequence is to ask: What is the lesson here?

A teaching consequence is often one of three types:

• Natural consequence: what naturally follows (when safe).

• Logical consequence: connected to the behavior (cleaning up, repairing, replacing).

• Relational repair: restoring trust (apology, making amends, re-doing the moment).

A shame consequence attacks the child's identity ("You're bad," "You're dramatic," "What's wrong with you?"). A teaching consequence addresses the behavior and the repair ("That hurt someone. We fix what we hurt.").

Discipline across lanes: cordial, parallel, protective

Your lane determines what discipline coordination can look like:

Cordial lane: You can talk. You can align on non-negotiables and a few shared routines. Use a monthly 20-minute check-in focused only on the child's needs.

Parallel lane: Keep it structured. Share only what is necessary for consistency (bedtime rhythm, school expectations, safety rules). Use BIFF-style messages: brief, informative, calm.

Protective lane: If safety is at risk, discipline conversations are not the priority—protection is. Increase supervision and professional support. Document, follow required channels, and keep the child out of adult conflict.

Simple scripts (so you don't have to improvise under stress)

When you need to pause before correcting: "I'm getting worked up. I'm going to take a minute and we'll talk when I'm calm."

When you're naming the behavior without shaming: "You're not bad. That choice wasn't okay. Let's fix what happened and talk about what to do next."

When you're teaching repair: "What was the impact? What do you need to do to make it right?"

When the other adult is harsher than you prefer (cordial/parallel): "For the child's sake, can we focus on teaching and repair rather than shame? Let's agree on one consequence that helps them learn."

When the other adult is permissive and you're worried: "I'm seeing more dysregulation after transitions. Can we agree on one consistent boundary—bedtime rhythm or homework window—to help the child feel steady?"

To extended family who undermine: "We can disagree privately. In front of the child, we stay respectful and consistent."

If you're the one cleaning up: don't hand your bitterness to the child

In capacity-gap families, one adult often becomes the cleanup crew: the one who calms the child after a harsh moment, the one who rebuilds trust, the one who does the steady work.

If that's you, your anger makes sense. But kid-first wisdom asks you to relocate that anger to adult spaces—so your child doesn't learn contempt as a coping strategy.

Your child will be more stable if you help them hold two truths: "I can enjoy the good I get," and "I am still safe even when adults are inconsistent."

This is not pretending. It's protecting a child from being trained into bitterness.

A Small Step This Week
This week, choose one discipline change that your child will feel immediately.

Pick one:

- Adopt the triangle: Regulate → Guide → Connect (and write it where you can see it).

- Choose five non-negotiables and repeat them daily for one week.

- Replace one shame phrase with one teaching phrase (for example: swap "What is wrong with you?" for "What happened, and what do we do now?").

- Practice one repair the same day: "I'm sorry. I was too sharp. Let's try that again."

Small shifts practiced consistently build a child's confidence: "My adults can lead me without crushing me."

Next: we'll focus on transitions between homes—and keep translating kid-first values into daily, doable steps.

Closing prayer
God, teach me to shepherd, not shame.

Help me lead with calm authority—firm, loving, consistent.

When I feel triggered, help me pause and return regulated.

Give our family the gift of repair, so conflict does not become the story our child carries.

And let discipline be discipleship: steady guidance that forms wisdom over time.

Amen.

Kid-First takeaway: boundaries aren't punishment—they're protection. Teach with love, correct with calm, and reconnect after hard moments.

Chapter 8 Endnotes (APA 7th Edition)
1. Sege, R. D., & Siegel, B. S.; Council on Child Abuse and Neglect; Committee on Psychosocial Aspects of Child and Family Health. (2018). Effective discipline to raise healthy children.

Pediatrics, 142(6), e20183112.
https://doi.org/10.1542/peds.2018-3112

2. Gershoff, E. T., & Grogan-Kaylor, A. (2016).
Spanking and child outcomes: Old controversies
and new meta-analyses. Journal of Family
Psychology, 30(4), 453–469.
https://doi.org/10.1037/fam0000191

3. Siegel, D. J., & Bryson, T. P. (2011). The Whole-
Brain Child: 12 revolutionary strategies to nurture
your child's developing mind. Bantam.

4. Gottman, J., & DeClaire, J. (1997). Raising an
emotionally intelligent child. Simon & Schuster.

Chapter 9
Transitions Between Homes

What Transitions Feel Like to Children (by age)
Children don't experience transitions as logistics.
They experience them as safety, loss, loyalty, and
belonging. Use the age lens below to choose the
simplest supports that match your child's stage.

- Ages 0–5: Your calm body is the plan. Keep
  goodbyes short, repeat the same phrases, and
  protect sleep and meals. Expect clinginess and
  big feelings after the switch.

- Ages 6–11: Kids want predictability and
  fairness. Use a visual calendar, a consistent
  packing routine, and a short "reset" ritual when
  they arrive (snack, shower, quiet play).

- Ages 12–18: Teens need dignity and agency.
  Offer choices inside boundaries ("Do you want
  to unpack now or after dinner?"). Keep
  questions gentle; let them decompress before
  talking.

- All ages: Don't make the transition a debrief of
  the other home. Lead with connection ("I'm
  glad you're here") before corrections.

How to reduce the emotional whiplash of handoffs and help kids settle

Transitions are where a lot of families unravel

If there is one place co-parenting stress shows up fast, it's the handoff.

Transitions between homes are emotionally loaded moments: a child is shifting environments, rules, expectations, routines, and sometimes loyalties. Adults are often carrying their own history into the doorway, too.

So it makes sense that pickups and drop-offs become the stage where tension leaks—sharp tone, passive comments, long speeches, last-minute changes, guilt, or conflict in the driveway.

Kid-first co-parenting treats transitions as sacred ground: we protect them on purpose.

Different ages, different needs

Child development research reminds us that what children need in custody and access arrangements depends heavily on their age and developmental stage—especially for very young children who rely on routine, familiar caregiving, and predictable soothing to feel safe.1

You don't need to memorize developmental theory. You just need to remember this: transitions should match the child's capacity, not the adults' convenience.

Why kids may melt down at the door
Many children don't melt down because they are "being difficult." They melt down because their nervous system is shifting gears.

Some children act out at the handoff because they feel torn—loving both homes and not knowing how to hold that tension.

Some children regress because change activates emotional security needs. When the system feels shaky, behavior is often the language of stress.

Research on emotional security emphasizes that children's adjustment is shaped not only by the family structure, but by how safe and stable the interparental environment feels—especially during conflict-laden moments.4

The Transition Formula: brief, calm, child-centered
If you only remember three words for handoffs, remember these: brief, calm, child-centered.

- Brief: Keep adult interaction short. The longer adults linger, the more tension can leak.

- Calm: Neutral tone. No sarcasm. No coldness. No performance.

- Child-centered: The child is not the messenger. The child is not the audience for adult emotion.

A kid-first transition is not the time for:

- discipline debates

- schedule negotiations

- emotional speeches

- guilt trips or "tell your mom/dad…" messages

- questioning the child about the other home

The 10-minute settle (a small ritual that changes everything)

Most kids need a short "settle" window after a transition. Think of it as emotional decompression.

You don't need a big talk. You need a small ritual that tells the child's nervous system: you are safe here.

Try this for the first 10 minutes after the handoff:

- Connection first: eye contact, greeting, warmth. "I'm glad to see you."

- Snack or hydration (many kids melt down because their body is low).

- One predictable question: "What do you need first—quiet, a hug, or to play?"

- No interrogation about the other home.

- Then move into the routine: unpack, wash hands, settle into the next rhythm.

If you do nothing else, do this: protect the first ten minutes. They set the emotional tone for the whole evening.

Scripts that keep the doorway clean
At the door (cordial): "Thanks. Have a good evening."

At the door (parallel): "Okay. See you Sunday at 5:30."

If the other adult tries to argue: "Not here. We can message later. Keeping this calm for the child."

If the child is melting down: "You're safe. We'll take this one step at a time. You don't have to choose."

If you need to end the exchange: "We're going to head in now. We'll follow up by text."

Logistics that reduce stress
When homes are changing, small logistics can carry big emotional weight. Reduce friction where you can.

Kid-first logistics include:

- A packed "always bag" with essentials (to reduce last-minute conflict).

- A shared calendar (if cordial) or clear written schedule (if parallel).

- Clear drop-off and pickup locations (neutral when needed).

- No surprise changes unless truly urgent.

When transitions are high-conflict or unsafe
Some families need more than scripts. They need protection.

If transitions have become hostile, unpredictable, or unsafe, consider kid-first protective options:

- Neutral exchange locations (school, daycare, supervised visitation centers when appropriate).

- Third-party exchange support (trusted adult) to reduce adult contact.

- Written-only communication about logistics.

- Professional support to structure and monitor the plan.

Across the family-court literature, a consistent theme is that child outcomes are shaped not just by where children spend time, but by the level of conflict and the quality of the plan that supports stability and parent functioning.2

Helping children hold two homes in one heart
Children do best when they are not forced to split their heart.

They can love two homes. They can miss one parent while being with the other. They can enjoy time without being disloyal.

Your job is to give them permission for that wholeness.

If your child feels anxious or sad during transitions, don't rush to "fix" the feeling. Name it and normalize it:

"That makes sense. Switching homes can feel big. We're going to take it slow and steady."

Programs designed to support children and caregivers through divorce and high-stress family transitions often emphasize coping skills, stable routines, and reduced conflict exposure—and have shown positive effects on child outcomes in rigorous evaluations.3

A Small Step This Week
This week, choose one transition change that protects the child's nervous system.

Pick one:

- Adopt the "brief, calm, child-centered" rule at every handoff.

- Protect the first 10 minutes after arrival (connection, snack, predictable routine).

- Stop asking questions about the other home for one week. If a child wants to share, listen—without interrogating.

- Create an "always bag" to reduce last-minute conflict.

Chapter 9 Endnotes (APA 7th Edition)

1. Kelly, J. B., & Lamb, M. E. (2000). Using child development research to make appropriate custody and access decisions for young children. Family and Conciliation Courts Review, 38(3), 297–311.

2. Lamb, M. E. (2012). Critical analysis of research on parenting plans and children's well-being. In L. Drozd, M. Saini, & N. Olesen (Eds.), Parenting plan evaluations: Applied research for the family court (pp. 214–242). Oxford University Press.

3. Sandler, I. N., Tein, J. Y., Wolchik, S., & Ayers, T. S. (2016). The effects of the New Beginnings Program on children and adolescents. Prevention Science, 17(1), 75–86.

4. Davies, P. T., & Cummings, E. M. (1994). Marital conflict and child adjustment: An emotional security hypothesis. Psychological Bulletin, 116(3), 387–411.

In the pages ahead: we'll focus on kid-first decision framework—and keep translating kid-first values into daily, doable steps.

Children settle faster when transitions are predictable. And when children settle faster, adults fight less. It's a mercy loop.

Closing prayer
God, help me keep the doorway clean.

Give me a calm spirit and a gentle tongue when it would be easy to leak tension onto this child.

Help me protect transitions with wisdom—brief, kind, and steady.

Teach my child's nervous system that home can be safe, even when life is complicated.

And let peace be the legacy we hand them, one transition at a time.

Amen.

Kid-First takeaway: the handoff is not just a schedule change—it is a nervous system change. Make it predictable, calm, and kind.

Chapter 10
Kid-First Decision Framework

A simple filter for messy moments—so children aren't carrying adult chaos

The main thing
The main thing is building a stable, loving environment where children can thrive—no matter how complicated the family structure becomes.

When adults stay grounded and intentional, children can grow with greater peace, security, and confidence—even in imperfect and painful circumstances.

This chapter gives you a simple decision framework you can return to when your emotions rise and your options feel unclear.

Because kid-first parenting is often not about having perfect choices. It's about choosing the option that reduces chaos and increases safety.

Research consistently links ongoing interparental conflict and children feeling "caught" between adults with higher risk for child adjustment difficulties—reinforcing the kid-first goal of reducing conflict exposure and keeping children out of adult roles.12

Stress becomes especially harmful when it is intense, frequent, and unsupported—what child-development science often describes as toxic stress.3

This framework is designed to help you lower toxic stress patterns and replace them with stability.

A note about honoring an unwell or inconsistent parent

There are seasons when a parent, due to instability, illness, addiction, or limited emotional capacity, is unable to fulfill the role of parenting in a consistent way.

Kid-first care helps you accomplish the main thing while still honoring that parent with dignity and compassion.

Honoring someone does not mean ignoring reality or sacrificing safety. It means telling the truth with love, setting wise boundaries, and creating stability where it is possible.

Before you decide: Pause and name the moment (30–60 seconds)

When tension rises, decisions get rushed. Use this short pause before texting, reacting, or making changes:

When you feel rushed or reactive, use the 30–60 second pause to name the moment. You'll find the full pause prompts and the complete Kid-First Filter in Appendix A (so you can keep it printed or screenshotted).

Kid-First Filter: The 7 Questions

Before you decide, slow down: run the decision through the seven Kid-First questions. If anything feels unclear, pause and get support (full list in Appendix A).

1) Safety: Does this protect the child physically, emotionally, and spiritually?

2) Stability: Will this reduce disruption and increase predictability (routines, schedules, expectations)?

3) Belonging: Does this help the child feel loved and secure in both homes (or in the home they live in)?

4) Respect: Does this avoid putting the child in the middle or asking them to carry adult messages?

5) Development: Is this age-appropriate, and does it support the child's long-term growth?

6) Peace: Will this lower conflict exposure for the child (even if it doesn't make adults happy)?

7) Legacy: Will this decision help build a story the child can be proud of later?

Honor-with-Boundaries Check (when a caregiver is unstable)
Use this section when instability affects parenting. It helps you hold compassion and clarity at the same time.

- Honor: Can I speak about the caregiver with dignity, without covering harm or pretending things are okay?

- Truth: Am I naming reality clearly (to myself, to my supports, and when needed, to professionals)?

When a caregiver is unwell or unreliable, you'll need compassion and clarity at the same time. Use the Honor-with-Boundaries Check in Appendix A to decide what's safest right now—and to keep your language dignified in front of children.

- Support: Who needs to be involved (counselor, pastor, medical care, legal support) to keep the child safe?

Choose your lane: Cordial, Parallel, or Protective
Not every family can co-parent the same way in every season. Choose the lane that best protects the

child's peace and stability right now (see Appendix A for a quick summary).

- Cordial lane: communication stays respectful, so you can coordinate calendars, discuss needs, and solve problems together.

- Parallel lane: communication is minimal and structured; each home runs its routine with clear boundaries to reduce conflict exposure for the child.

- Protective lane: when safety is at risk, boundaries tighten and support increases; you prioritize safety and stability over togetherness.

Quick scripts (use them—don't over-explain)
Put simply: To the other caregiver (parallel): "I'm going to keep communication brief and focused on logistics. Please send updates by text/email."

When you're unsure: the three-step reset
When you feel stuck, do three simple things:

When you're unsure, don't escalate. Use the simple three-step reset (Appendix A): pause if you can, consult one steady voice, then choose the decision that builds stability.

What we'll tackle next: we'll focus on protecting kids from adult weight—and keep translating kid-first values into daily, doable steps.

Why this filter matters long-term

This framework isn't about perfection. It's about reducing preventable stressors that accumulate over time. Large-scale public health research has linked adverse childhood experiences and chronic household dysfunction with later health and mental health risks.4

Current public health guidance emphasizes preventing and buffering adversity through stable relationships, safe environments, and supportive systems—exactly what kid-first co-parenting is trying to build.5

Closing prayer

God, keep me anchored to the main thing—the child's stability and peace.

Give me wisdom to build stability and tender strength for these children, even when the adults are strained, wounded, or divided.

Put simply: Teach me to honor people with dignity while also telling the truth and setting boundaries that protect what is sacred.

Give me courage to choose peace over pride, and faith to believe that steady love can still shape a legacy—even in a complicated story.

Amen.

Kid-First takeaway: the win is a child who feels loved, safe, and protected—while adult problems stay in adult hands.

Chapter 10 Endnotes (APA 7th Edition)

1. van Eldik, W. M., Luijk, M. P. C. M., Parry, L. Q., & Prinzie, P. (2020). The interparental relationship: Meta-analytic associations with children's maladjustment and responses to interparental conflict. Psychological Bulletin, 146(7), 553–594. https://doi.org/10.1037/bul0000233

2. Schrodt, P. (2025). Interparental conflict and parent–child triangulation: A meta-analytical review of children feeling caught between parents. Human Communication Research. Advance online publication. https://doi.org/10.1093/hcr/hqaf018

3. Harvard University, Center on the Developing Child. (n.d.). Toxic stress. https://developingchild.harvard.edu/science/key-concepts/toxic-stress/

4. Felitti, V. J., Anda, R. F., Nordenberg, D., et al. (1998). Relationship of childhood abuse and household dysfunction to many of the leading causes of death in adults. The Adverse Childhood Experiences (ACE) Study. American Journal of Preventive Medicine, 14(4), 245–258.

5. Centers for Disease Control and Prevention. (n.d.). Preventing adverse childhood experiences (ACEs). https://www.cdc.gov/violenceprevention/aces/

Chapter 11
Protecting Kids From Adult Weight

How to tell the truth without turning your child into your confidant

Children can survive hard truths. They can't survive being the adult.

One of the most damaging patterns in complicated families is not divorce, or single parenting, or kinship care.

It is role reversal: when the child becomes the emotional support for the adult.

This can happen loudly—through arguments in the home. It can also happen quietly—through oversharing, venting, private details, or treating a child like a "little friend" who understands the adult world.

Most adults don't mean to do it. It often comes from loneliness, exhaustion, and a desperate need to be seen.

But kid-first co-parenting is clear: children are not built to hold adult burdens.

The middle is not a place a child should live

Research on triangulation and children feeling "caught" between parents shows that being pulled into adult conflict is associated with increased distress and negative adjustment outcomes for children.1

Sometimes the child is the messenger: "Tell your dad…" "Ask your mom…"

Sometimes the child is the spy: "What did they say about me?"

Sometimes the child is the judge: "Who do you want to live with?"

Sometimes the child is the therapist: listening to adult pain, mediating adult fights, reassuring an adult who can't regulate.

Sometimes the child is the emotional spouse: filling an adult's loneliness and becoming the adult's main comfort.

All of these put a child in the middle. And the middle is a heavy place.

A simple family-systems truth: clear boundaries protect children

Family therapy has long emphasized the importance of appropriate boundaries between adults and children.

When boundaries blur, children become responsible for roles they cannot carry—emotionally, developmentally, spiritually.

In healthy systems, adults turn toward other adults for adult needs. Children turn toward adults for safety and care.

Structural family therapy describes how boundary problems can create enmeshment and role confusion—where children function in adult roles and lose protected childhood space.2

Intergenerational family therapy also highlights the burden of loyalty conflicts—children feeling responsible to manage fairness, guilt, or emotional debt between adults.3

Why adult weight shows up in a child's body
Children don't just "hear" adult stress. They absorb it.

When children live in emotional unpredictability or role confusion, their nervous system adapts for survival—hypervigilance, anxiety, control, shutdown, people-pleasing.

That adaptation can look like "maturity." But it is often stress in a suit.

Research on childhood adversity suggests that threat-related stressors (like conflict, fear, and instability) and deprivation-related stressors (like emotional unavailability) can shape brain development and stress physiology in distinct ways.4

At the same time, resilience research reminds us that stable, supportive relationships are one of the strongest protective factors for children—what some researchers call "ordinary magic."5

So the goal is not to create a stress-free world. The goal is to make sure the child has at least one stable adult relationship where they do not have to carry adult weight.

Truth-telling without oversharing
Kid-first families tell the truth in age-appropriate ways. They do not build fantasy stories. They do not create shame stories either.

Here is the simplest rule: children need clarity, not details.

Clarity answers: "Am I safe? Is this my fault? Who is taking care of me? What happens next?"

Details often answer the adult's need to be understood. That need belongs with adults.

Three levels of truth (what a child can hold)
When you're deciding what to say, think in three levels:

Level 1: Safety truth What the child needs to know to feel safe and understand the plan.

Level 2: Emotional truth Naming feelings without blaming: disappointment, sadness, mixed emotions.

Level 3: Adult detail History, betrayal, mental health details, legal details—adult spaces only.

Most kids thrive with Level 1 and Level 2 truth. Level 3 truth belongs in adult circles.

Kid-first scripts for common moments
When a child asks why a parent didn't show up: "I don't know all the reasons, but I know this: it's not your fault. The plan is ___, and you are safe and loved."

When a child feels loyalty pressure: "You don't have to choose. You're allowed to love both caregivers."

When a child repeats adult accusations: "That sounds like adult conversation. You don't have to carry that. If you have feelings, I'm here."

When you feel tempted to vent to your child: "I need to talk to another adult about my feelings. Thank you for telling me how you feel—your feelings matter."

To extended family who overshare: "We're keeping adult details out of the child's world. Please talk to me privately."

Build an adult outlet plan (so kids aren't the outlet)

If you are going to protect your child from adult weight, you must have somewhere else to put it.

This is not weakness. It is responsible leadership.

Create a short list of adult outlets:

- One safe friend or mentor who can hold your truth without stirring drama.

- One professional support (therapist, counselor, pastor) when possible.

- One practice that regulates your body (walking, prayer, breathwork, exercise, journaling).

- One boundary that reduces reactivity (24-hour pause rule; BIFF texts only; no arguments at transitions).

When adults have outlets, children get their childhood back.

A Small Step This Week

This week, choose one way you will protect your child from adult weight.

Pick one:

- Stop messages through the child (100%—no exceptions).

- Remove adult venting from car rides (use music, audiobooks, or quiet instead).

- Choose one "adult outlet" and schedule it this week (call, session, meeting).

- Practice Level 1 and Level 2 truth with your child—clarity without details.

This is not about being perfect. It's about guarding what is sacred: a child's protected space to grow.

Closing prayer

God, forgive me for the times I have handed my child what I should have carried as an adult.

Give me wisdom to tell the truth with love—clear, age-appropriate, steady.

Help me build adult supports so my child does not become my outlet.

Protect this child's heart from loyalty pressure and adult conflict.

And let our home be a refuge where childhood can breathe again.

Amen.

Kid-First takeaway: safety is not negotiable. When risk is present, structure and support come before togetherness.

Chapter 11 Endnotes (APA 7th Edition)

1. Schrodt, P. (2025). Interparental conflict and parent–child triangulation: A meta-analytical review of children feeling caught between parents. Human Communication Research. Advance online publication. https://doi.org/10.1093/hcr/hqaf018

2. Minuchin, S. (1974). Families and family therapy. Harvard University Press.

3. Boszormenyi-Nagy, I., & Spark, G. M. (1973). Invisible loyalties: Reciprocity in intergenerational family therapy. Harper & Row.

4. McLaughlin, K. A., Sheridan, M. A., & Lambert, H. K. (2014). Childhood adversity and neural development: Deprivation and threat as distinct dimensions of early experience. Neuroscience & Biobehavioral Reviews, 47, 578–591.

5. Masten, A. S. (2014). Ordinary magic: Resilience in development. Guilford Press.

Chapter 12
The Age of the Wound

Why adults regress under stress—and how regulated caregiving changes everything

When adults get activated, they often get younger

If you have ever thought, "Why did I react like that?" you are not alone.

Most adults don't choose immaturity on purpose. Many of us are simply unaware of what happens in the nervous system under stress.

When a present-day moment presses against an old wound, we can temporarily respond from the age we were when the wound first formed.

In psychology and trauma work, this is often described as emotional regression: a return to earlier coping patterns when the nervous system senses danger.

When Grief and Trauma Show Up in Children

Kids often show grief and trauma sideways. A child may seem "fine" at school and fall apart at home, or act angry when they are actually scared. Regression, sleep disruption, stomachaches, clinginess, shutdown, and risk-taking can be the language of nervous system overload—not defiance.

- Name the feeling, not the story: "That was a big day. Your body seems tense. I'm here."

- Keep routines boring (in a good way): predictable meals, sleep, and school reduce nervous system threat.

- Repair quickly after ruptures: kids heal in relationship. A calm apology from an adult is powerful trauma prevention.

- Get support when symptoms persist: a child therapist, school counselor, or pediatrician can help you assess what's going on.

This chapter is not here to diagnose anyone. It is here to give you language for a common human experience—so you can stop shaming yourself and start building skill.

What regression can look like (without anyone meaning harm)
• The calm adult becomes controlling when they feel powerless.

• The rational adult becomes explosive when they feel disrespected.

• The steady adult becomes silent and withdrawn when conflict rises.

• The compassionate adult becomes sharp and shaming when fear for the child gets loud.

To the outside observer, these reactions can look dramatic or immature. But often they are the nervous system doing what it learned long ago to survive.

The nervous system explanation (in plain language)

When the brain senses threat, the body prepares for survival. Heart rate increases. Stress hormones rise. Attention narrows. The goal becomes immediate protection, not thoughtful problem-solving.

In those moments, the parts of the brain responsible for reflection and flexible thinking are less accessible, and the survival system takes the lead.

This is why you can "know better" and still react worse.

Trauma research describes how the body can store threat responses long after a danger has passed, keeping the system on alert and easily activated.1

Neurodevelopmental models also describe how chronic stress can leave "islands" of immature regulation—parts of the system that respond as if the past is still present.2

Interpersonal neurobiology emphasizes integration: helping different parts of the mind and brain connect so present-day wisdom can guide present-day responses.3

Why co-parenting triggers are so intense
Co-parenting conflict is not just an "argument." For many adults, it activates attachment fears: abandonment, betrayal, shame, helplessness, being unseen, losing control of the child's safety.

When attachment fear rises, the nervous system moves into protection mode. Some people fight. Some flee. Some freeze. Some fawn (people-please) to keep the peace.

Understanding this does not excuse harmful behavior. It explains why skill is needed—not just willpower.

Polyvagal theory offers a useful lens here: when the body senses safety, we can connect and reason; when it senses threat, we shift into defensive states that make calm communication harder.4

Kid-first co-parenting takes this seriously because children don't just hear our words—they feel our nervous systems.

From reaction to restoration: a two-step question

When you feel yourself escalating, ask two questions:

1) How old do I feel right now?

2) What does the younger part of me believe is about to happen?

This does not mean you become self-absorbed. It means you become self-aware.

Self-awareness is what makes self-control possible.

Regulation is a skill, not a personality trait

Some people grew up with adults who modeled calm repair. Others grew up with chaos, silence, or fear. So regulation does not come equally naturally to everyone.

But regulation can be learned. It can be practiced. It can be strengthened like a muscle.

And because children borrow regulation before they build it, adult skill-building is one of the most child-protective forms of love.

A kid-first regulation skill set (borrowed from evidence-based practice)

One of the most well-known evidence-based skill models for emotional regulation is Dialectical Behavior Therapy (DBT), which teaches practical skills for distress tolerance, emotion regulation, and interpersonal effectiveness.5

You do not need a full DBT program to benefit from the basic principles. Here are kid-first adaptations you can use immediately:

- Name the state: "I'm activated." (Naming reduces shame and increases choice.)

- Change the body: slow breathing, cold water on the face, a short walk—anything that tells the body, "We are safe."

- Delay the decision: "I'm going to pause and come back."

- Choose one wise action: the next step that lowers conflict exposure for the child.

- Repair quickly: "I missed it. I'm sorry. Let's try again."

How this changes co-parenting

When you understand the age of the wound, you stop being surprised by adult regression. You start planning for it.

You learn your triggers. You learn your patterns. You build boundaries around your nervous system: when you respond, how you respond, what you do before you speak.

You also become more compassionate without becoming permissive. You can say, "I see that this is hard," and still say, "This behavior is not safe or acceptable."

Most importantly, you stop asking your child to absorb the fallout of adult regression.

A note for helpers: compassion plus structure
If you are a pastor, therapist, mentor, or family support person reading this, the goal is not to talk families into calm. The goal is to build practices that make calm more possible.

Compassion without structure often enables chaos. Structure without compassion often creates shame. Kid-first care holds both.

A Small Step This Week
This week, do three things:

In the next chapter: we'll focus on honor without enabling—and keep translating kid-first values into daily, doable steps.

- Identify one trigger that reliably activates you (a tone, a text, a transition, a feeling of being dismissed).

- Choose one body-based regulation practice you will use before responding (breath, walk, prayer, cold water, grounding).

- Write one repair sentence you will use when you miss it: "I'm sorry. That was my stress talking. You are safe."

These small steps are not minor. They are how a child learns that adults can be safe even when life is stressful.

Closing prayer
God, meet me at the age of my wound.

Give me compassion for my own nervous system without excusing my harmful reactions.

Teach me to pause, to breathe, to return to wisdom when fear gets loud.

Help me become a steady adult so this child does not carry what I haven't healed.

Restore the years the locust has eaten, and make my home a place where peace can grow.

Amen.

Kid-First takeaway: the win is a child who feels loved, safe, and protected—while adult problems stay in adult hands.

Chapter 12 Endnotes (APA 7th Edition)

1. van der Kolk, B. A. (2014). The body keeps the score: Brain, mind, and body in the healing of trauma. Viking.

2. Perry, B. D., & Szalavitz, M. (2006). The boy who was raised as a dog: And other stories from a child psychiatrist's notebook. Basic Books.

3. Siegel, D. J. (2012). The developing mind: How relationships and the brain interact to shape who we are (2nd ed.). Guilford Press.

4. Porges, S. W. (2011). The polyvagal theory: Neurophysiological foundations of emotions, attachment, communication, and self-regulation. W. W. Norton.

5. Linehan, M. M. (2015). DBT skills training manual (2nd ed.). Guilford Press.

Chapter 13
Honor Without Enabling

How to speak with dignity about an inconsistent caregiver while protecting the child

The hardest place to stay mature is the place you've been hurt

If you are the one who keeps showing up, you may carry a quiet resentment that feels justified.

You're not wrong for feeling it. You have likely carried more weight than you should have had to carry.

But kid-first co-parenting asks a holy, difficult question:

What will my child inherit from my pain—bitterness or steadiness?

This chapter is for the caregivers who are doing the work while someone else cannot—or will not.

We are going to talk about honor without enabling: dignity without denial, compassion without chaos.

Honor is not denial

Honoring an inconsistent caregiver does not mean pretending everything is fine.

It does not mean giving access that isn't safe. It does not mean letting a child be repeatedly disappointed without protection.

Honor means you speak with basic dignity, you tell the truth with love, and you build boundaries that protect what is sacred: the child's safety and emotional steadiness.

Enabling is different. Enabling is when we cover reality, excuse harm, or keep handing a child the same disappointment with no plan.

Kid-first care holds both compassion and clarity at the same time.

Why contempt is a burden for children
When adults speak with contempt about the other caregiver, children often feel caught: loving one adult feels like betraying the other. This loyalty pressure is a known stressor for children in conflict systems.1

Even when children are angry at the inconsistent caregiver, they rarely benefit from being trained into contempt. Contempt makes their world smaller and more divided.

Kid-first wisdom doesn't ask you to lie. It asks you to avoid recruiting your child into adult judgment.

Give your child two truths they can live inside

Most children become more stable when they are allowed to hold two truths at the same time:

Truth one: "I can enjoy the good I get with that caregiver."

Truth two: "I am still safe and cared for even when that caregiver is inconsistent."

When kids are allowed to hold both, they stop feeling like they have to split their heart.

Structure is how you protect a child from repeated disappointment

If a caregiver is inconsistent, the kid-first answer is not repeated hopeful guessing. It is a plan.

A plan does three things:

• It reduces last-minute chaos.

• It protects the child from adult volatility.

• It gives the child language for disappointment that doesn't become shame.

This is where earlier chapters connect: minimum viable plans, transition rules, written schedules, and a circle of care are not cold—they are compassionate.

Studies of post-separation family interventions show that improving co-parenting quality—reducing undermining and increasing supportive, structured cooperation—can benefit child adjustment outcomes.2

What to say (truth with love, no diagnosis)
Your child does not need adult explanations. Your child needs clarity and safety. Try these scripts:

When a caregiver cancels: "I'm sorry. I know that hurts. It's not your fault. We have a plan for today, and you are safe."

When the child is angry: "It makes sense to feel angry. You don't have to hide that. We can talk about your feelings without tearing anyone down."

When the child has a good visit: "I'm glad you enjoyed that time. You're allowed to enjoy it."

When the child worries about the caregiver: "It's kind that you care. Adults are responsible for adult choices. Your job is to be a kid, and my job is to keep you safe."

When extended family tries to stir bitterness: "We can talk privately. In front of the child, we keep it respectful and steady."

Where to put your anger and grief

If you don't give your grief an adult container, it will leak into the child's world.

This is not a moral failure. It is a human reality.

So kid-first care builds an adult container on purpose:

• One person who can hear your truth without escalating drama.

• One practice that regulates your body when resentment rises.

• One boundary that keeps you from processing in front of the child.

Resilience research consistently highlights the protective power of stable, supportive relationships—especially at least one steady adult who provides warmth, structure, and reliable "return" when a child reaches out.3

Developmental science often describes this as "serve and return": the back-and-forth responsiveness that builds secure brain circuitry and a sense of safety.4

When you keep showing up steadily, you are doing more than being "the responsible one." You are literally building safety inside the child.

Honor-with-Boundaries checklist

Use this checklist when you feel torn between compassion and protection:

- Dignity: Can I speak respectfully without pretending?

- Reality: What is consistently happening over time (not what is promised)?

- Access is a safety decision, not a guilt decision. For some seasons that means full contact; for others it means supervised, limited, or paused contact—based on what protects the child's stability right now (see Appendix A for the full Honor-with-Boundaries Check).

- Stability: What routines must be protected no matter what?

- Support: What adult supports do I need so I don't leak resentment onto the child?

- Repair: How will I help the child process disappointment without building contempt?

A steady boundary script (DEAR-style, simplified)

When boundaries are hard, it helps to use a simple interpersonal template. DBT teaches structured communication skills to ask for what you need while staying regulated.5

Try this simplified version:

- Describe (facts): "The last three pickups were canceled within an hour."

- Express (briefly): "That creates stress for the child."

- Ask (clear): "Please confirm by 3:00 p.m. if you're coming."

- Boundary (firm): "If I don't have confirmation, we will follow the backup plan."

This is not punishment. It is predictability.

A Small Step This Week
This week, choose one honor-with-boundaries step.

Next: we'll focus on when safety is at risk—and keep translating kid-first values into daily, doable steps.

Pick one:

- Replace one contempt phrase with a dignity phrase in front of the child.

- Create a written backup plan for cancellations (what the child can expect).

- Schedule one adult outlet for your grief (counseling, pastor, mentor).

- Practice the "two truths" language with your child: enjoy the good; safe in the hard.

Your child's stability does not require your silence. It requires your maturity.

Closing prayer

God, help me honor people with dignity without denying reality.

When resentment rises, give me adult places to put my pain so my child is not the container.

Teach me to speak truth with love, to set boundaries with courage, and to build stability with faithfulness.

Let my child inherit steadiness more than bitterness—peace more than pressure.

Amen.

Kid-First takeaway: the win is a child who feels loved, safe, and protected—while adult problems stay in adult hands.

Chapter 13 Endnotes (APA 7th Edition)
1. Schrodt, P. (2025). Interparental conflict and parent–child triangulation: A meta-analytical review of children feeling caught between parents.

Human Communication Research. Advance online publication. https://doi.org/10.1093/hcr/hqaf018

2. Sandler, I. N., Wolchik, S. A., Winslow, E., Mahrer, N. E., Moran, J. A., Weinstock, D., & Schenck, C. (2012). Quality of coparenting and child adjustment after divorce: A randomized trial. Journal of Consulting and Clinical Psychology, 80(4), 706–717.

3. Masten, A. S. (2014). Ordinary magic: Resilience in development. Guilford Press.

4. Center on the Developing Child at Harvard University. (n.d.). Serve and return interaction shapes brain circuitry. https://developingchild.harvard.edu/science/key-concepts/serve-and-return/

5. Linehan, M. M. (2015). DBT skills training manual (2nd ed.). Guilford Press.

Chapter 14
When Safety Is at Risk

Protective parenting for hard situations—without handing kids more fear

When to Get Help Now (a gentle red-flags list)
This list is not meant to scare you. It is meant to reduce confusion. If any of these are present, pause the debate and get local professional help right away.

- Unexplained injuries, repeated bruises, or a child expressing fear about going to a caregiver.

- Threats, stalking, intimidation, or behavior that makes you afraid to set boundaries.

- A caregiver driving under the influence, active intoxication, or unsafe supervision (young children left alone, weapons unsecured, dangerous people in the home).

- Severe mental health instability without a safety plan (psychosis, suicidal behavior, violent outbursts).

- Neglect patterns: chronic lack of food, hygiene, supervision, medical care, or school attendance.

If you believe a child is in immediate danger, follow your local emergency procedures immediately.

Kid-first begins with safety

Some chapters in this book are about improving cooperation. This chapter is about something more urgent: protection.

There are situations where the kid-first pathway is not "better communication." It is increased structure, increased supervision, and appropriate professional involvement.

If you are reading this chapter because you are worried a child is being harmed, neglected, or placed in unsafe situations, I want to say this clearly:

You are not overreacting for taking safety seriously.

Kid-first always begins with safety—physical, emotional, and spiritual.

A careful note about scope

This is not legal advice, and it cannot replace local guidance from professionals and authorities in your area.

But it can give you a kid-first framework: what to prioritize, what not to do in panic, how to reduce fear for the child, and how to build a plan that holds.

If you believe a child is in immediate danger, contact emergency services in your region.

Why safety concerns require clarity—not denial or drama

Public health guidance emphasizes that child maltreatment is preventable and that protective action often depends on early recognition, stable caregiving, and connecting families to support systems.1

Global prevention frameworks also emphasize that violence against children is reduced through safe environments, caregiver support, and systems that respond when danger is present.5

Kid-first protective parenting holds two truths at once: we don't minimize risk, and we don't recruit children into panic.

What "safety risk" can look like

Safety concerns vary widely, and they do not all require the same response. But kid-first wisdom begins by naming what is observable and what impacts the child.

Examples include:

- Unexplained injuries or patterns of injury.

- Unsafe supervision (a child left alone, driven by impaired adults, exposed to violence).

- Threats, intimidation, or severe emotional aggression in the home.

- Severe impairment that prevents basic caregiving (consistent inability to provide food, hygiene, school attendance, medical care).

- Credible fear expressed by a child, or clear signs of trauma response following visits or exposure.

You do not have to label or diagnose an adult to take a child's reality seriously. Name the child's reality and respond with appropriate protection.

The kid-first protective response (five steps)
When you suspect harm or unsafe conditions, this sequence helps you stay steady:

1) Stabilize the child first (safety, calm, basic needs).

2) Document facts (dates, times, what you observed—not interpretations).

3) Seek appropriate professional evaluation and guidance.

4) Limit risk exposure (tighten boundaries, supervised contact when needed).

5) Protect the child from adult conflict and interrogation.

Step 3: get professional eyes on the situation
Clinical guidance emphasizes that suspected physical abuse should be evaluated carefully and systematically—often involving medical professionals trained to assess injuries and patterns.2

If there are injuries, seek medical evaluation from a pediatric clinician as soon as possible. Medical documentation matters, and it also protects you from relying on guesses.

If there is ongoing concern or conflict about what happened, child advocacy models often use specialized, trained professionals and coordinated systems designed to reduce repeated questioning and to protect the integrity of the child's report.

Child Advocacy Centers (CACs) are one coordinated model in many regions for forensic interviewing and multidisciplinary response when abuse is suspected.3

Your job is not to be the investigator. Your job is to be the safe adult who responds wisely.

How to talk to a child without interrogating
When adults are scared, we often ask too many questions. We want clarity. We want proof. We want to know what happened.

But kids can become overwhelmed, confused, or pressured—especially if they feel they have to choose a side.

Kid-first communication with a child is simple: calm presence, open-ended space, and reassurance.

Kid-first guidelines:

- Stay calm. Your nervous system teaches their nervous system what is happening.

- Use open-ended invitations: "Tell me what happened," rather than leading questions.

- Don't promise secrecy. Promise support: "I'm glad you told me. I'm going to help keep you safe."

- Avoid repeating the story multiple times. Let trained professionals do formal interviewing when needed.

Simple scripts:

When a child shows you an injury: "Thank you for telling me. I'm going to make sure your body is okay and you're safe."

When a child is scared: "You are safe with me right now. We're going to get help from grown-ups whose job is to protect kids."

When a child worries about "getting someone in trouble" : "Adults are responsible for adult choices. Your job is to tell the truth and be a kid."

Protective parenting is a lane, not a punishment
When safety is at risk, you may need to move into protective parenting.

Protective parenting is not revenge. It is not payback. It is not a statement about someone's worth.

It is a temporary lane designed to reduce risk exposure while the situation is clarified and stabilized.

Protective parenting may include supervised contact, neutral exchanges, written-only communication, and increased professional involvement.

If the other caregiver is unsafe, your job is not to negotiate your child into danger. Your job is to protect the child while the adult situation is addressed.

For the protective caregiver: fear and anger are normal—don't let them drive the car

When safety is threatened, your protective instincts will surge. Anger is normal. Fear is normal. Shock is normal.

Kid-first wisdom doesn't shame those emotions. It asks you to regulate them so your child doesn't have to.

Your child needs a steady adult more than they need a perfectly calm adult. When you feel yourself escalating, return to basics:

- Breathe and slow your body (even 60 seconds helps).

- Call one steady adult (pastor, counselor, mentor) so you're not alone.

- Keep communication factual and written when possible.

- Do not argue in front of the child—ever.

If a child is traumatized: steady care plus the right support

Not every scary situation becomes long-term trauma, but children do best when adults respond with steadiness and supportive help.

One evidence-based therapy model for children who have experienced trauma is Trauma-Focused Cognitive Behavioral Therapy (TF-CBT). It is designed to help children process traumatic experiences safely with caregiver involvement.

TF-CBT is widely described in clinical literature as an effective treatment approach for many children with trauma-related symptoms.4

Kid-first support at home includes:

- Keep routines as predictable as possible (sleep, meals, school).

- Offer extra co-regulation: warmth, presence, reassurance, and calm structure.

- Normalize feelings: "It makes sense to feel scared/sad/confused."

- Avoid pushing for details. Let professionals lead formal assessment when needed.

A Small Step This Week
Do three things:

1. Make a written safety-and-coverage plan for the next 7 days (who supervises, who transports, who is the backup).

2. Choose written, factual communication only for logistics.

3. Schedule one support appointment for the child and one for you (professional or pastoral)—so neither of you carries this alone.

The child does not need to see you win. The child needs to see you protect.

Closing prayer
God, make me brave and steady when a child's safety is at stake.

Give me wisdom to act with clarity, not panic; with truth, not denial; with courage, not revenge.

Protect this child's body, mind, and spirit.

Surround them with safe adults and wise helpers.

And help our family choose the pathway that keeps what is sacred protected.

Amen.

Kid-First takeaway: safety is not negotiable. When risk is present, structure and support come before togetherness.

Chapter 14 Endnotes (APA 7th Edition)
1. Centers for Disease Control and Prevention. (n.d.). Preventing child abuse and neglect. https://www.cdc.gov/violenceprevention/childabus eandneglect/

2. Christian, C. W.; Committee on Child Abuse and Neglect. (2015). The evaluation of suspected child physical abuse. Pediatrics, 135(5), e1337–e1354. https://doi.org/10.1542/peds.2015-0356

3. National Children's Alliance. (n.d.). Standards for accredited members / child advocacy center model. https://www.nationalchildrensalliance.org/

4. Cohen, J. A., Mannarino, A. P., & Deblinger, E. (2017). Trauma-focused CBT for children and adolescents: Treatment applications. Guilford Press.

5. World Health Organization. (2020). INSPIRE: Seven strategies for ending violence against children. https://www.who.int/publications/i/item/9789240021024

In the pages ahead: we'll focus on teaching regulation to kids—and keep translating kid-first values into daily, doable steps.

If you arc in a safety-concern season, your first week goal is stabilization, not perfection.

Chapter 15
Teaching Regulation to Kids

Co-regulation, routines, and repair—so children don't inherit adult chaos

Regulation is the hidden curriculum of childhood

When families are complicated, children often learn two lessons at the same time: how to love, and how to brace.

They learn to read the room. They learn to predict tone. They learn to manage adults—sometimes more than adults manage themselves.

Kid-first co-parenting is not only about reducing conflict. It's also about giving children skills and environments that help their nervous systems settle.

Here is the simplest truth in child development: kids learn regulation through relationship.

Before children can calm themselves, they borrow calm from us.

Many parenting frameworks describe this process as co-regulation: adults providing steady presence, structure, and emotional naming so a child's brain can integrate feeling with thinking.1

Emotion coaching approaches likewise emphasize helping children identify feelings, accept them without shame, and choose wise behavior—skills linked to stronger long-term emotional competence.2

This chapter is practical: what to do in the moment, what to build over time, and how to stay kid-first even when you are tired.

Why complicated families create bigger feelings
Children in two-home or high-stress systems often carry extra emotional load:

• uncertainty ("What happens next?")

• loyalty pressure ("Will someone be upset if I enjoy the other home?")

• grief ("Why isn't it normal?")

• hypervigilance ("What mood will I walk into?")

So it is normal to see more dysregulation at transitions, bedtime, school mornings, and after adult conflict—whether the child heard it directly or simply felt the atmosphere.

Pediatric and developmental science describes how chronic, unsupported stress can become toxic stress—shaping learning, behavior, health, and emotional development over time.3

Your job is not to eliminate all stress. Your job is to buffer it with steadiness, connection, and predictable care.

The Regulation Ladder: body → feelings → choices

When a child is dysregulated, many adults try to start with logic: "Calm down." "Use your words." "Stop it."

But dysregulated brains don't learn well from lectures. So we climb a ladder in the right order:

1) Body first: help the nervous system settle.

2) Feelings next: name what's happening inside.

3) Choices last: teach the skill or boundary and practice the repair.

This is consistent with the idea that regulation begins as a physiological process and becomes a cognitive skill over time.5

Body-first tools (fast and simple)

When a child is escalated, start with one of these:

- Lower your voice and slow your body (kids mirror speed).

- Offer water or a snack (hunger and thirst look like behavior).

- Change the environment: step outside, move rooms, dim lights.

- Use movement: wall push-ups, jumping jacks, a short walk.

- Use grounding: "Tell me five things you see. Four things you feel."

- Use comfort: a hug if welcomed, a weighted blanket, a quiet corner.

You are not "rewarding bad behavior" by helping a child's body settle. You are creating the conditions where learning becomes possible.

Feelings next: name it without making it bigger
Once the child's body is settling—even a little— help them name what is happening.

Try this three-part sentence:

"I see ___ (emotion). It makes sense because ___. And we're going to ___ (next step)."

Examples:

- "I see you're angry. It makes sense because transitions are hard. We're going to breathe and then unpack."

- "I see you're sad. It makes sense because you miss them. We're going to sit together for a minute, and then we'll make a plan for tonight."

- "I see you're overwhelmed. It makes sense because mornings feel rushed. We're going to slow down and do one step at a time."

Choices last: boundaries that teach

After regulation and naming, we teach the skill or boundary.

Kid-first boundaries are firm and calm. They don't threaten. They don't shame. They don't require the child to become "fine" to be loved.

Teach in small pieces:

- Name the limit: "I won't let you hit."

- Name the skill: "You can stomp your feet or squeeze this pillow."

- Practice the redo: "Let's try that again with your words."

- Repair if needed: "What do we do to make it right?"

Routines are regulation in disguise

A child's nervous system calms faster when life has predictable rhythms.

This is why bedtime routines, morning routines, and transition rituals matter so much in complicated families. They reduce uncertainty.

You don't need perfect routines. You need repeatable routines.

Try building three regulation routines:

- A transition ritual (first 10 minutes: connection + snack + settle).

- A bedtime rhythm (same order; calm ending; screens rest).

- A repair rhythm (when conflict happens: name, apologize, restore, reconnect).

Repair teaches security

Children become more secure when they learn that hard feelings don't break relationships—and that adults can own mistakes and return to love.1

A kid-first repair has four parts:

- Name what happened (briefly).

- Own your part (no excuses).

- Name the plan (what will change).

- Reconnect (warmth and presence).

Repair scripts you can use:

When you were too sharp: "I'm sorry. I was frustrated and I spoke too sharply. That wasn't your job to carry. I'm going to try again."

When the child was dysregulated: "That was a big moment. You're not in trouble for having feelings. We're learning what to do with them."

After a hard transition: "We made it through. I'm proud of you. Let's reset."

When caregivers differ: don't weaponize regulation

In co-parenting systems, one adult may be more skilled at regulation than another.

Kid-first wisdom says: don't use that difference to shame. Use it to stabilize.

Your child does not benefit from, "Your other caregiver is why you're like this."

Your child benefits from, "Big feelings are normal. We're learning skills."

If you can align with the other caregiver, align on two things:

• a shared calm-down routine (what to do when dysregulated)

• a shared repair routine (what to do after conflict)

What we'll tackle next: we'll focus on rebuilding trust and repairing ruptures—and keep translating kid-first values into daily, doable steps.

A Small Step This Week

This week, do one small regulation upgrade:

- Create a Calm Corner (blanket, pillow, book, sensory item) and teach your child how to use it when calm.

- Practice the three-part sentence once per day: "I see ___; it makes sense because ___; and we're going to ___."

- Choose one routine to protect (bedtime or transition) and keep it consistent for seven days.

- Practice one repair the same day you miss it.

Skill grows through repetition. And in complicated families, repetition is love.

Closing prayer

God, help me be a steady presence to a child with big feelings.

Teach me to lead with calm authority—firm, gentle, and consistent.

Give me wisdom to build routines that create peace, and patience to practice skills again and again.

When I miss it, help me repair quickly so my child learns that love returns.

Let our home be a place where emotions are safe and children can grow strong.

Amen.

Kid-First takeaway: calm is contagious. Your regulated presence teaches your child's brain what safety feels like.

Chapter 15 Endnotes (APA 7th Edition)
1. Siegel, D. J., & Bryson, T. P. (2011). The Whole-Brain Child: 12 revolutionary strategies to nurture your child's developing mind. Bantam.

2. Gottman, J., & DeClaire, J. (1997). Raising an emotionally intelligent child. Simon & Schuster.

3. Shonkoff, J. P., Garner, A. S.; Committee on Psychosocial Aspects of Child and Family Health; Committee on Early Childhood, Adoption, and Dependent Care; Section on Developmental and Behavioral Pediatrics. (2012). The lifelong effects of early childhood adversity and toxic stress. Pediatrics, 129(1), e232–e246. https://doi.org/10.1542/peds.2011-2663

4. Perry, B. D., & Szalavitz, M. (2006). The boy who was raised as a dog: And other stories from a child psychiatrist's notebook. Basic Books.

5. Gross, J. J. (2015). Emotion regulation: Current status and future prospects. Psychological Inquiry, 26(1), 1–26.
https://doi.org/10.1080/1047840X.2014.940781

Chapter 16
Rebuilding Trust and Repairing Ruptures

How to come back after hard seasons—without making the child prove anything

Repair is not an event. It's a pattern.
Every complicated family has ruptures: missed visits, broken promises, harsh words, seasons of absence, court stress, illness, addiction, conflict that got too loud.

Some adults want to rush to "moving on." Some kids want to pretend nothing happened. Some adults want the child to forgive quickly so the adult feels better.

Kid-first repair is slower and steadier than that.

Repair is not a speech. It's a pattern of safety rebuilt over time.

This chapter is about how trust returns: through consistent care, honest repair, and predictable boundaries.

Why trust matters to a child's nervous system
Trust is not just an emotion. It is a body-level expectation: "When I need you, you will respond."

Attachment research emphasizes that secure relationships are built through responsiveness, emotional availability, and repair after rupture—not through perfection.

Attachment-focused clinical work highlights that bonding is strengthened when caregivers can recognize distress, respond with attunement, and repair relational breaks.13

Interpersonal neurobiology likewise emphasizes that the developing mind is shaped by relationships—especially repeated experiences of being seen, soothed, and reconnected after disconnection.4

So when a child has lived through rupture, the kid-first question becomes: What experiences will teach their body that love returns?

What not to do after a rupture
When adults feel guilt or shame, they often reach for strategies that backfire:

- Oversharing adult explanations to the child.

- Demanding forgiveness or closeness on the adult's timeline.

- Buying closeness (gifts, screen time, permissiveness) instead of building safety.

- Interrogating the child: "Are you okay now?" "Do you love me again?"

- Minimizing: "That wasn't a big deal."

Children should never have to perform emotional reassurance so an adult can feel okay.

The Trust Staircase: presence → predictability → protection → partnership

Trust returns like a staircase, not like a light switch. Here is a simple way to build it:

1) Presence: Show up in small, consistent ways. Don't disappear emotionally.

2) Predictability: Keep routines. Confirm plans. Do what you say you will do.

3) Protection: Set boundaries that keep the child safe from adult volatility.

4) Partnership: As trust returns, invite the child into age-appropriate collaboration ("What helps you feel settled?").

If you skip steps, you may get short-term closeness and long-term anxiety. Kid-first repair stays on the staircase.

The repair conversation (short, honest, age-appropriate)

When a rupture has happened, children need two things: an honest naming, and a stable plan.

A kid-first repair conversation can be as short as four sentences:

- Name it: "That was hard."

- Own your part: "I didn't handle that well."

- Protect them: "That wasn't your responsibility."

- Plan it: "Here's what will be different next time."

Examples you can use:

After adult conflict exposure: "You saw us upset. I'm sorry. That wasn't your job to carry. We're going to talk away from you and keep transitions calm."

After a missed visit: "I know that was disappointing. You didn't cause it. The plan is ___, and we have a backup plan when adults don't follow through."

After your own sharp moment. "I was too sharp. I'm sorry. I'm going to take a pause when I'm overwhelmed so I can speak with respect."

Trust grows through consistency, not intensity

Some adults try to rebuild trust with intensity: big talks, big promises, big weekend plans, big emotions.

Children often feel overwhelmed by intensity. They feel safe with consistency.

So the kid-first strategy is simple: small consistent promises you keep.

A promise you can keep is more powerful than a promise you wish you could keep.

Repair between adults protects children—even when kids never hear the details

Sometimes the rupture is between co-parents: broken agreements, conflict, mistrust.

Even if the adults never become close, repair can still happen through clarity and follow-through.

This is where structured tools matter: BIFF communication, written schedules, and a return to non-negotiables.

When adults can re-stabilize their working relationship, children breathe easier.

Relationship research commonly highlights the importance of repair attempts—small bids to de-escalate and reconnect—when conflict arises.2

When a child resists closeness (and why that can be healthy)
After rupture, some children become clingy. Others become distant. Others become angry.

Distance is not always disrespect. Sometimes it is a child's way of staying safe: "If I don't need you, you can't hurt me."

Kid-first parenting does not punish self-protection. It offers steady presence without pressure.

You can say, "I'm here," without demanding, "Come close."

When children carry chronic stress, some may develop anxiety, depression, or behavior problems; careful support and stable relationships are protective across developmental outcomes.5

A Small Step This Week
This week, rebuild trust with one small staircase step:

- Presence: 10 minutes of undistracted connection each day (no fixing, just being).

- Predictability: one promise you can keep every day this week (bedtime story, pickup time, a check-in).

- Protection: one boundary that reduces conflict exposure (no arguing at transitions; written-only logistics).

- Partnership: ask one question: "What helps you feel safe when things are hard?"

Trust is rebuilt when children experience you as steady—not when they hear you as sorry.

Closing prayer
God, help me rebuild what has been cracked.

Give me humility to own my part, courage to set wise boundaries, and patience to let trust return on a child's timeline.

Teach me to show up consistently—in small ways that add up to safety.

And let repair become a pattern in our home, so children learn that love returns after hard moments.

Amen.

Kid-First takeaway: the win is a child who feels loved, safe, and protected—while adult problems stay in adult hands.

Chapter 16 Endnotes (APA 7th Edition)

1. Johnson, S. M. (2019). Attachment theory in practice: Emotionally focused therapy (EFT) with individuals, couples, and families. Guilford Press.

2. Gottman, J. M., & Gottman, J. S. (2017). The natural principles of love. Journal of Family Theory & Review, 9(1), 7–26. https://doi.org/10.1111/jftr.12182

3. Mikulincer, M., & Shaver, P. R. (2016). Attachment in adulthood: Structure, dynamics, and change (2nd ed.). Guilford Press.

4. Siegel, D. J. (2012). The developing mind: How relationships and the brain interact to shape who we are (2nd ed.). Guilford Press.

5. Wolff, J. C., & Ollendick, T. H. (2006). The comorbidity of conduct problems and depression in childhood and adolescence. Clinical Psychology Review, 26(1), 1–17.

Chapter 17
When Your Co-Parent
Is High-Conflict

Staying steady when someone else escalates—so the child doesn't live in warfare

Some co-parenting problems aren't disagreements. They're patterns.
Many co-parenting struggles can be improved with skill, support, and time.

But some situations are different. You are not arguing about bedtime. You are navigating a pattern of escalation: accusations, rapid-fire texts, last-minute sabotage, insults, threats, social media posts, or constant re-litigation of the past.

In these systems, the goal is not "getting on the same page." The goal is reducing the child's exposure to conflict and building a plan that holds even when the other adult does not cooperate.

Kid-first co-parenting does not require you to win a personality contest. It requires you to stay steady so the child is not living in warfare.

Define high-conflict by behavior, not by labels

We are not here to diagnose your co-parent. We are here to name observable patterns that impact the child.

High-conflict patterns often include:

- Frequent escalation over minor issues.

- All-or-nothing thinking (everything is an emergency, everything is betrayal).

- Undermining and triangulation (pulling the child into adult conflict).

- Boundary violations (showing up unannounced, contacting repeatedly, refusing agreed channels).

- Revision of history (denying prior agreements, re-framing facts to provoke debate).

- Public conflict (social media, extended family campaigns).

If you recognize these patterns, the kid-first move is not more explaining. It is more structure.

Structure is compassion for a child in a storm

In high-conflict systems, communication can become an emotional treadmill. You respond to the provocation, the provocation escalates, and the child feels the heat.

Kid-first care shifts the focus from persuasion to protection.

High-Conflict Reality Check
If communication repeatedly escalates, or if you feel intimidated, manipulated, or trapped in endless conflict loops, the goal shifts from "working it out" to "reducing exposure." High-conflict co-parenting often requires structure more than conversation.

- Use one-lane communication: brief, factual, and logistical. Avoid defending yourself by text. Reply on a schedule (e.g., once daily) unless there's a true emergency.

- Prefer written channels (email/text) over phone calls if calls lead to escalation. Keep messages child-focused and neutral.

- Set exchange boundaries: public locations, a neutral adult present when needed, and no "parking lot negotiations."

- If you are dealing with coercive control or threats, do not rely on goodwill. Get local professional guidance and prioritize protective boundaries.

You do not have to convince someone to be reasonable in order to build a reasonable plan.

Research across the divorce and family-conflict literature has long emphasized that children's adjustment is more strongly linked to the level of ongoing interparental conflict than to family structure alone.12

Four tools that reduce conflict exposure
These tools are simple, but they are not easy. They require discipline. They also protect children quickly.

1) One channel: Use one written channel for logistics (text/email/app). No phone arguments. No hallway debates.

2) BIFF responses: Brief, Informative, Friendly, Firm. One topic, one request, no bait-taking.

3) Boundaries with consequences: Not punishment—predictability. If you don't confirm by __, we follow the schedule. If you escalate, we pause and respond later.

4) Third-party structure: When needed: parenting coordination, mediation, supervised exchanges, or other local supports.

BIFF communication is a widely used practical model in high-conflict contexts for reducing escalation in written messages.4

Professional guidelines describe parenting coordination as one structured approach used in some high-conflict cases to help implement child-focused plans and reduce conflict exposure.3

Don't JADE: the trap that keeps you stuck
In high-conflict dynamics, many steady adults get pulled into the JADE trap: Justify, Argue, Defend, Explain.

JADE feels logical. It feels like you are clearing your name. It feels like you are finally going to be understood.

But in high-conflict patterns, JADE often fuels escalation because the goal is not understanding. The goal is engagement.

Kid-first wisdom says: stop feeding the fire. Respond to logistics, not to provocation.

Scripts that keep you out of the fire
When bait arrives: "I'm going to keep this focused on the child's logistics. Pickup remains 5:30."

When accusations come: "I'm not going to debate. Here is the plan for today."

When messages keep coming: "I've received your message. I will respond within 24 hours."

When they demand an immediate reply: "I will respond when I'm available. If it's urgent medical/safety, please state the urgent issue."

When extended family gets recruited: "We're keeping communication direct and child-focused. I'm not discussing this with others."

Protect transitions like a border
High-conflict adults often try to use the doorway as a stage. Don't give them one.

Use brief, calm, child-centered exchanges. Consider neutral locations or third-party exchanges when needed.

Your child should never have to watch adults perform power struggles.

Your nervous system is your strategy
When someone is high-conflict, they often feel contagious. Their urgency wants to become your urgency.

The most powerful kid-first skill in these systems is regulated non-engagement.

Regulated non-engagement does not mean passivity. It means you refuse to escalate.

In the next chapter: we'll focus on building the village—and keep translating kid-first values into daily, doable steps.

You do not match their intensity. You match your values.

Coparenting research frameworks describe how undermining, conflict, and poor coordination increase stress in the family system—reinforcing the child-protective value of structured, low-conflict patterns.5

A Small Step This Week
This week, choose one structural change that lowers conflict exposure:

- Move all logistics to one written channel and use BIFF only.

- Adopt a 24-hour response window for non-urgent messages.

- Write one boundary script and use it every time (no improvising).

- Protect transitions: brief handoffs, no discussion at the door.

- Choose one third-party support option available to you (pastor/therapist/mentor; mediation; parenting coordination).

Structure will feel cold at first if you are used to explaining. But to a child, structure feels like peace.

Closing prayer
God, make me steady when someone else is stormy.

Guard my mouth, my phone, and my heart from being pulled into escalation.

Give me courage to set boundaries that protect this child, and wisdom to use the supports available to us.

Let my child grow up breathing peace—not warfare.

Amen.

Kid-First takeaway: your child doesn't need you to win—they need you to lower the volume of adult conflict and raise the level of stability.

Chapter 17 Endnotes (APA 7th Edition)
1. Johnston, J. R., Campbell, L. E. G., & Mayes, S. S. (1985). Latent hostility and divorce: A developmental study of children. American Journal of Orthopsychiatry, 55(4), 556–567.

2. Saini, M., Drozd, L. M., & Olesen, N. W. (2017). Parenting plan evaluations: Applied research for the family court. Oxford University Press.

3. Association of Family and Conciliation Courts. (2019). Guidelines for Parenting Coordination. https://www.afccnet.org/Portals/0/Committees/Gu idelines%20for%20Parenting%20Coordination%20 2019.pdf

4. Eddy, B., Burns, A. T., & Chafin, K. (2020). BIFF for Coparent Communication: Your guide to difficult texts, emails, and social media posts. Unhooked Books/High Conflict Institute Press.

5. Feinberg, M. E. (2003). The internal structure and ecological context of coparenting: A framework for research and intervention. Parenting: Science and Practice, 3(2), 95–131.

Chapter 18
Building the Village

How to invite support without letting the village become another conflict

Sometimes kid-first is not "two parents." It's "one circle."

Many families I serve are not two-parent systems. Some children have one engaged parent. Some have grandparents stepping in. Some have foster or kinship care. Some have rotating caregivers because adults are inconsistent or overwhelmed.

If that is your reality, you are not disqualified from raising stable children. You simply need a different structure.

Kid-first co-parenting expands into kid-first caregiving: building a village that functions like a team.

But a village can either become a circle of care—or a crowd of opinions.

This chapter helps you build the circle.

Public child welfare guidance describes kinship care as relatives and trusted "fictive kin" stepping in when parents cannot provide safe, consistent care.1

Clinical and pediatric guidance also notes that kinship caregivers often carry significant stress and practical needs (financial, legal, medical, respite), and they benefit from coordinated support rather than assumptions.2

What the village is for (and what it is not for)
A kid-first village is for:

- stability and coverage (so the child is not dropped when adults are overwhelmed)

- consistent routines (so the child can predict life)

- safe relationship (so the child has at least one steady adult)

- buffering stress (so the child doesn't live in adult chaos)

A kid-first village is not for:

- deciding the child's future based on adult grudges

- re-litigating history in front of the child

- turning caregiving into a power contest

- recruiting the child into loyalty battles

Revisit the Circle of Care: roles create peace

If you read Chapter 5, you've already met the Circle of Care idea. Here we apply it to the village.

The fastest way to reduce village conflict is to clarify roles:

- Who is the Steady Care Team (Ring 1)?

- Who is the Practical Support Team (Ring 2)?

- Who is the Professional Team (Ring 3)?

When roles are unclear, everyone feels anxious—and anxiety often becomes control.

A Village Agreement (so helpers don't become harm)

If multiple adults are involved, write a short agreement. Keep it simple. Post it. Repeat it.

- We do not argue about caregiving in front of the child.

- We do not speak with contempt about any caregiver in front of the child.

- We follow one weekly plan and one pickup/drop-off rhythm.

- We keep discipline consistent on safety and respect, even if styles differ.

- We communicate through one channel and keep it child-focused.

- When adults disagree, we consult a steady third party rather than escalating in front of the child.

When the village is caring for a child with trauma

Many village-built families are also trauma-affected families: the child has lived through instability, loss, fear, or repeated disappointment.

Trauma-informed care does not mean walking on eggshells. It means building safety, predictability, and dignity into the child's world.

Trauma-informed frameworks emphasize understanding how stress and adversity shape responses and building environments that are safe, trustworthy, collaborative, empowering, and culturally responsive.[5]

Resilience research consistently highlights that children do better when they have stable, supportive relationships and protective systems—even when their stories include hardship.[3]

Developmental science also emphasizes "serve and return" responsiveness—reliable back-and-forth care that helps children build secure circuitry for regulation and connection.[4]

A village becomes protective when it offers consistent return: adults respond, return, and repair rather than disappear, dismiss, or explode.

How to ask for help without shame
Many caregivers carry shame about needing help. Especially grandparents and single parents. Especially those in church communities who feel they should "have it together."

But kid-first care reframes help as wisdom: children are not meant to be raised by one overwhelmed adult.

Ask clearly. Ask specifically. And ask for roles— not vague rescue.

Examples of clear asks:

- "Can you cover pickup every Wednesday for the next month?"

- "Can you be our backup adult if a visit cancels last-minute?"

- "Can you sit with us once a week and help us keep the plan steady?"

- "Can you pray with me and check in twice a week so I don't leak stress onto the child?"

Next: we'll focus on partnering with schools and professionals—and keep translating kid-first values into daily, doable steps.

Protect the child from village conflict

If your village fights, narrow the circle. A child needs fewer adults who are steady, not more adults who are loud.

Kid-first caregiving often means disappointing some people so the child can have peace.

Remember this: stability is not built by consensus. It is built by consistency.

A Small Step This Week

This week, build one piece of your village on purpose:

- List Ring 1, Ring 2, and Ring 3 supports (names and numbers).

- Write a one-week coverage plan with one backup adult.

- Choose one communication rule for the village: "We keep adult conflict out of the child's hearing."

- Make one specific ask for help (role + time + frequency).

A village becomes healing when it is organized around the child—not around adult pride.

Closing prayer
God, expand the circle around this child with safe love.

Give me humility to ask for help, wisdom to organize support, and courage to set boundaries when the village becomes noise.

Bless the caregivers who are stepping in. Strengthen the weary. Calm the reactive. Heal what is broken.

And let this child grow up held—not by chaos, but by steady hands.

Amen.

Kid-First takeaway: children thrive when adults are aligned. Clarify roles, protect routines, and keep adult resentment out of the child's ears.

Chapter 18 Endnotes (APA 7th Edition)
1. Child Welfare Information Gateway. (n.d.). Kinship care. U.S. Department of Health and Human Services, Administration for Children and Families, Children's Bureau. https://www.childwelfare.gov/topics/permanency/kinship-care/

2. Rubin, D., Springer, S. H., Zlotnik, S., Kang-Yi, C. D., & Council on Foster Care, Adoption, and Kinship Care. (2017). Needs of kinship care families and pediatric practice. Pediatrics, 139(4), e20170099. https://doi.org/10.1542/peds.2017-0099

3. Masten, A. S. (2014). Ordinary magic: Resilience in development. Guilford Press.

4. Center on the Developing Child at Harvard University. (n.d.). Serve and return interaction shapes brain circuitry. https://developingchild.harvard.edu/science/key-concepts/serve-and-return/

5. Substance Abuse and Mental Health Services Administration. (2014). SAMHSA's concept of trauma and guidance for a trauma-informed approach (HHS Publication No. SMA14-4884). https://store.samhsa.gov/product/SAMHSA-s-Concept-of-Trauma-and-Guidance-for-a-Trauma-Informed-Approach/SMA14-4884

Chapter 19
Partnering With Schools and Professionals

How to build a child-centered team with teachers, counselors, pastors, and providers

Kid-first families don't "go it alone"
When family life is complicated, the child is often carrying invisible complexity into very ordinary places: school, daycare, church, sports, doctor visits, sleepovers, birthdays.

Teachers may see behavior changes without knowing why. Pediatric providers may see stomachaches or sleep issues without seeing the stress behind them. Pastors may see anxiety in a child long before anyone calls it that.

Kid-first co-parenting invites a simple shift:

You don't just need two adults to cooperate. You need a team around the child that is aligned on stability.

This chapter helps you build that team without oversharing, without stirring conflict, and without turning professionals into weapons.

Decades of research on family–school partnerships emphasize that children do better when schools and caregivers communicate, coordinate expectations, and build trust—especially when a child's life outside school includes stressors or transitions.12

Partnership does not mean telling everyone everything. It means giving the right people the right information so the child is supported.

Who can be on a child-centered team
Your child's team may include:

- School: teacher, counselor, school psychologist, principal (as needed).

- Health: pediatrician, therapist, psychiatrist, occupational therapist, speech therapist (as needed).

- Support: pastor, youth leader, mentor, trusted family support.

- Systems: caseworker, guardian ad litem, attorney, parenting coordinator/mediator (as applicable).

Not every child needs every role. The point is to stop leaving support to chance.

Three kid-first principles: clarity, consent, containment

Clarity: Share what the child needs supported (routines, triggers, transitions), not adult history.

Consent: When possible, get appropriate permissions for sharing information and keep it consistent across caregivers.

Containment: Keep adult conflict out of professional spaces. Professionals are for support, not for battles.

What to share with school (and what not to share)

Most schools need a short, practical summary—not a family narrative.

What to share (kid-first):

- Current schedule structure (two homes, transitions days).

- Any predictable stress points (Mondays after transition, court dates, changes in living situation).

- What helps the child regulate (snack, quiet corner, a movement break, check-in with counselor).

- Who is authorized to pick up the child and who receives school communication.

- One sentence goal: "We're building stability and limiting conflict exposure."

What not to share (adult-centered):

- Detailed accusations, adult betrayals, or legal strategy.

- Diagnostic labels or private medical details that are not necessary for the child's support plan.

- Extended family drama or social media narratives.

- Anything you would not want repeated in a school hallway.

A trauma-informed posture: assume stress before defiance

In complicated families, a child's behavior can change fast: more tears, more irritability, more shutdown, more control, more acting out.

That does not mean the child is "bad." It often means the child is stressed.

A trauma-informed approach helps adults respond with curiosity, safety, and structure rather than punishment-first escalation.

Trauma-informed guidance emphasizes building safety, trust, collaboration, empowerment, and consistent routines—protective factors that apply in schools, churches, and homes.3

How to work with a child's therapist without turning therapy into a battleground

Therapy can be one of the strongest supports for children in complicated systems—when adults protect it.

Here are kid-first ground rules for therapy:

- Don't use therapy as a courtroom. A therapist is not there to pick sides; they are there to help the child.

- Ask for skill-building, not verdicts: "Can we help my child with transitions and regulation?"

- Keep adult venting out of the child's session. Adult processing belongs in adult sessions.

- If co-parents are both involved, agree (when possible) on how updates will be shared so therapy doesn't become another conflict arena.

Partnering with pediatric providers

Pediatric providers often see the physical side of stress: headaches, stomachaches, sleep problems, appetite changes, regression.

When you share a short kid-first picture, a pediatric provider can better screen, guide, and refer when needed.

Pediatric guidance frameworks (including Bright Futures) emphasize routine psychosocial screening and family support as part of whole-child health.5

Partnering with pastors and mentors (pastoral care as a stabilizing force)
Pastors, mentors, and church leaders can be a stabilizing voice when they stay child-centered.

The goal is not to take sides. The goal is to protect the child's peace and support the adults toward maturity.

If you invite a pastor or mentor into the story, give them a clear assignment:

• help me stay regulated,

• help me keep communication child-centered,

• help our village stay respectful in front of the child.

When you need structured systems support
In some families, informal teamwork is not enough. Conflict is too intense, or agreements are not followed.

In those cases, structured supports can protect the child by creating clearer boundaries and processes.

Scripts you can use (school, therapist, pastor)
Email to a teacher/counselor: "Our family schedule includes transitions on ___. You may notice big feelings after change days. What helps is a brief check-in and a predictable routine. Please send school communication to ___."

To a therapist: "Our goal is stability and regulation for the child. Can we focus on transition skills and coping tools?"

To a pastor/mentor: "I need help staying steady so my child doesn't carry my stress. Can you check in with me weekly and help me stay kid-first?"

When someone asks for details you shouldn't share: "I'm keeping adult details private. What matters is the child's stability, and we're building support around that."

A Small Step This Week
This week, build one piece of the child's team:

- Send one kid-first email to the school with the practical items only (schedule, authorized contacts, what helps).

- Choose one professional or pastoral support for you (so your child isn't your outlet).

- Create a one-page "Child Support Summary" you can share when needed (routine, triggers, calming tools, key contacts).

Support becomes stable when it is organized. Organization is not cold—it's protective.

Closing prayer
God, surround this child with wise and steady helpers.

Give me humility to ask for support, discernment to share what is needed, and courage to keep adult conflict out of spaces meant for care.

Bless teachers, counselors, providers, pastors, and mentors who show up with compassion and clarity.

And let our child experience what it feels like to be held by a community that chooses peace.

Amen.

Kid-First takeaway: the win is a child who feels loved, safe, and protected—while adult problems stay in adult hands.

Chapter 19 Endnotes (APA 7th Edition)
1. Epstein, J. L. (2011). School, family, and community partnerships: Preparing educators and improving schools (2nd ed.). Westview Press.

2. Christenson, S. L., & Reschly, A. L. (Eds.). (2010). Handbook of school-family partnerships. Routledge.

3. Substance Abuse and Mental Health Services Administration. (2014). SAMHSA's concept of trauma and guidance for a trauma-informed approach (HHS Publication No. SMA14-4884). https://store.samhsa.gov/product/SMA14-4884

4. National Association of School Psychologists. (2020). The school psychologist's role in promoting family–school partnerships. https://www.nasponline.org/resources-and-publications/resources-and-podcasts/family-school-partnerships

5. American Academy of Pediatrics. (n.d.). Bright Futures: Guidelines for health supervision of infants, children, and adolescents (selected guidance on psychosocial screening and family support). https://brightfutures.aap.org/

6. Association of Family and Conciliation Courts. (2019). Guidelines for parenting coordination. https://www.afccnet.org/Portals/0/Committees/Guidelines%20for%20Parenting%20Coordination%202019.pdf

In the pages ahead: we'll focus on a child's story and your legacy—and keep translating kid-first values into daily, doable steps.

Professional guidelines describe parenting coordination as one structured approach used in some high-conflict cases to help implement child-focused plans and reduce repeated conflict exposure.6

Chapter 20
A Child's Story and Your Legacy

How to help children make meaning—without rewriting reality

Every child grows up inside a story
Children don't only grow up inside homes and schedules. They grow up inside meaning.

They are constantly asking questions, even if they don't say them out loud:

"Why is my family like this?" "Is it my fault?" "What does love mean?" "Can people be trusted?" "What happens when life breaks?"

Kid-first co-parenting is not just about managing logistics. It is about shaping the story a child will carry into adulthood.

And here is the good news: a complicated story can still become a strong story.

Meaning-making is part of development
Psychological work on narrative identity emphasizes that people make sense of their lives through story—how they interpret events, assign meaning, and integrate hardship into a coherent sense of self.1

Family narrative research also suggests that the way families talk about their history—truthfully, with warmth and coherence—can support children's identity and resilience over time.2

This does not mean you can control your child's interpretation. It means you can give them a healthier foundation to interpret from.

Three stories children often write (and how adults influence them)
In complicated families, children commonly drift toward one of these internal stories:

1) The Shame Story: "Something is wrong with me. I caused this. I'm too much."

2) The Contempt Story: "People are bad. Love is unreliable. I can't trust anyone."

3) The Resilience Story: "Hard things happened, and I was still loved. I can grow."

Adults don't write these stories for children, but adults powerfully influence which story feels true.

Protect your child from the Shame Story
Shame grows in confusion and silence. Kids fill in the blanks with self-blame.

So kid-first care gives children consistent clarity:

• This is not your fault.

- You are not responsible for adult choices.

- You are safe and cared for.

Clarity is not oversharing. It is naming what the child needs to know to feel safe.

Protect your child from the Contempt Story
Contempt grows when adults recruit children into bitterness.

Children may have real anger, and we can honor it. But we don't train them to despise a caregiver or to treat love as a joke.

Kid-first care says: we can tell the truth without tearing people down.

Your child benefits when they are allowed to appreciate any good they receive, while still being protected from what is unsafe.

Help your child build a Resilience Story
Resilience research emphasizes that children can do well even after adversity when protective factors are present—especially supportive relationships, routines, and opportunities to develop coping skills.35

Interpersonal neurobiology likewise highlights how relationships shape the developing mind and support integration—helping children connect feelings, meaning, and behavior in healthy ways.4

A resilience story usually includes three elements:

- Truth: "Hard things happened."

- Love: "I was still loved and protected."

- Growth: "I learned skills and I can build a good life."

Practical ways to shape a healthier story
You do not need long talks. You need repeated messages and experiences:

- Name strengths you see: "You're brave." "You're kind." "You keep trying."

- Tell coherent truth (age-appropriate): "Our family has two homes, and we're building stability."

- Celebrate small stability wins: "We handled that transition well."

- Practice gratitude without denial: "We can be thankful for the good and honest about the hard."

- Invite meaning through faith: "God is with us, and He can redeem what is broken."

Faith and meaning: redemption without pretending

As Christians, we believe God can redeem what is broken. That is not sentimental optimism—it is anchored hope.

Redemption does not require you to rewrite history. It requires you to live forward with truth and love.

You can say to your child, "This is not what we wanted, but God is with us, and we will build a life marked by peace."

What we'll tackle next: we'll focus on the 30-day kid-first reset—and keep translating kid-first values into daily, doable steps.

You are helping your child learn a theology of reality: lament and hope together.

Kid-first scripts for meaning-making

When a child asks, "Why is my family like this?" "Families can be complicated. Adults make choices, and sometimes adults struggle. What I want you to know is: it's not your fault, you're loved, and we have a plan."

When a child says, "I wish it was normal." "I understand. I wish it was easier too. And we can still build a good life with love and stability."

When a child feels embarrassed: "You don't have to be ashamed. Your story is not your failure. You are brave."

A Small Step This Week
This week, choose one story-building practice:

- Say "not your fault" out loud once a day for a week (kids need repetition).

- Name one strength you see in your child each day.

- Start a simple "wins" habit: one sentence at bedtime about what went well today.

- If faith is part of your home, pray a short stabilizing prayer with your child: "God, help us be safe and steady today."

Children build meaning from repetition.
Repetition is where hope becomes believable.

Closing prayer
God, help my child carry a story marked by truth and love.

Protect them from shame and bitterness.

Give me wisdom to speak with clarity, to live with steadiness, and to model hope without pretending.

Redeem what is broken, strengthen what is fragile, and let peace become part of our legacy.

Amen.

Kid-First takeaway: the win is a child who feels loved, safe, and protected—while adult problems stay in adult hands.

Chapter 20 Endnotes (APA 7th Edition)

1. McAdams, D. P. (2013). The redemptive self: Stories Americans live by (Revised and expanded ed.). Oxford University Press.

2. Fivush, R., Bohanek, J. G., & Duke, M. (2008). The intergenerational self: Subjective perspective and family history. In F. Sani (Ed.), Self continuity: Individual and collective perspectives (pp. 131–143). Psychology Press.

3. Masten, A. S. (2014). Ordinary magic: Resilience in development. Guilford Press.

4. Siegel, D. J. (2012). The developing mind: How relationships and the brain interact to shape who we are (2nd ed.). Guilford Press.

5. Center on the Developing Child at Harvard University. (n.d.). Resilience. https://developingchild.harvard.edu/science/key-concepts/resilience/

Chapter 21
The 30-Day Kid-First Reset

A practical way to move from overwhelm to stability—one week at a time

If you are overwhelmed, you are not failing—you are carrying too much

Complicated families often live in chronic triage. You put out today's fire, then tomorrow brings another.

So it makes sense if you have read this far and thought, "This is good… but where do I start?"

This chapter is your starting line.

Not a perfect plan. A real one.

A 30-day reset doesn't fix everything, but it can change the atmosphere in a home. It can give a child's nervous system a break. It can help adults move from reactive to intentional.

Behavior change research consistently shows that simple, specific plans ("If X happens, I will do Y") increase follow-through—especially under stress.[1]

Habit research also reminds us that change happens through repetition over time; consistency builds automaticity.[2]

So this reset is built on small, repeatable actions—because kids are shaped by what happens repeatedly, not occasionally.

The reset rules (keep it simple)

For the next 30 days, commit to these five rules:

1) Keep the doorway clean (no conflict at transitions).

2) Keep kids out of adult weight (no messages through the child; no venting to the child).

3) Protect two routines (bedtime + one other rhythm).

4) Use one communication lane (cordial, parallel, or protective) and stay in it.

5) Repair quickly when you miss it.

You can add more later. For now, these five create a foundation.

Week 1: Stabilize the nervous system (yours and theirs)

Goal: reduce emotional whiplash in the home.

Choose one adult regulation tool and one child regulation tool and use them every day.

Adult tools (pick one):

- 24-hour pause for non-urgent responses.

- A 5-minute walk before replying to stressful messages.

- Breathing prayer: inhale "Lord, have mercy," exhale "make me steady."

- A text rule: no responding when angry; draft, save, return later.

Child tools (pick one):

- The first 10-minute settle after transitions (connection + snack + routine).

- A calm corner and a simple script: "Feelings are safe here."

- One predictable bedtime rhythm (same order, calm ending).

Week 2: Build structure (so the child can predict life)

Goal: replace chaos with predictability.

Structure is not strictness. It is stability.

This week, build two documents:

1) One-week coverage plan (who does what, and what happens when plans fall through).

2) One-page house rules that hold (your top 5–7 rules: safety, respect, two routines).

Parent training and intervention literature consistently emphasizes that clear expectations and consistent follow-through support child behavior and family functioning.3

You are not building a perfect family system. You are building something your child can count on.

Week 3: Reduce conflict exposure (communication and transitions)

Goal: lower the child's exposure to adult conflict—especially during handoffs and texts.

Choose your lane (cordial, parallel, protective) and commit to one communication pattern for seven days.

Your Week 3 commitments (pick three):

- Use BIFF-style messages only: brief, informative, friendly, firm.

- Use one channel only (email/text/app).

- No talking at transitions beyond "hello/thank you."

- No schedule changes without confirmation in writing.

- A weekly 15-minute kid-focused check-in (cordial lane only).

If you feel tempted to explain, remember: in high stress systems, structure protects children faster than persuasion.

Week 4: Repair and meaning (so the child's story becomes strong)

Goal: teach the child that hard moments don't destroy love—and that adults return to steadiness.

This week, practice two repairs:

• one adult-to-child repair (when you are sharp or stressed),

• one home repair rhythm (after conflict, after a transition, after disappointment).

Adult-to-child repair script:

"I'm sorry. That was my stress talking. You are safe and loved. I'm going to try again."

Home repair rhythm (simple):

- Name: "That was hard."

- Own: "I didn't handle that well."

- Plan: "Next time I will pause before I speak."

- Reconnect: "Come sit with me; we're okay."

Programs designed to support families through separation and stress often emphasize skill-building, reduced conflict exposure, and supportive parenting practices—elements linked to improved child outcomes.4

Resilience science consistently points to stable relationships and supportive environments as protective factors—even when adversity is real.5

If you miss a day, don't restart—return
Most families quit because they think a missed day means failure.

Kid-first growth is not a streak. It's a return.

If you miss it, return to the simplest reset: protect transitions, protect routines, keep kids out of adult weight, repair quickly.

A child does not need a perfect adult. A child needs an adult who returns to love.

A one-sentence commitment (write it down)
Write one sentence and put it where you will see it:

"For the next 30 days, I will choose stability over winning—so my child can breathe."

Closing prayer
God, give me grace for the parts of this story I cannot control.

Give me courage for the parts I can.

Help me build stability in small, faithful steps—so this child does not carry what adults haven't resolved.

Teach me to return to love quickly when I miss it, and to trust that steady care can change a family atmosphere over time.

Amen.

Kid-First takeaway: the win is a child who feels loved, safe, and protected—while adult problems stay in adult hands.

Chapter 21 Endnotes (APA 7th Edition)

1. Gollwitzer, P. M. (1999). Implementation intentions: Strong effects of simple plans. American Psychologist, 54(7), 493–503. https://doi.org/10.1037/0003-066X.54.7.493

2. Lally, P., van Jaarsveld, C. H. M., Potts, H. W. W., & Wardle, J. (2010). How are habits formed: Modelling habit formation in the real world. European Journal of Social Psychology, 40(6), 998–1009. https://doi.org/10.1002/ejsp.674

3. Kazdin, A. E. (2005). Parent management training: Treatment for oppositional, aggressive, and antisocial behavior in children and adolescents. Oxford University Press.

4. Sandler, I. N., Tein, J. Y., Wolchik, S., & Ayers, T. S. (2016). The effects of the New Beginnings Program on children and adolescents. Prevention Science, 17(1), 75–86.

5. Center on the Developing Child at Harvard University. (n.d.). Resilience. https://developingchild.harvard.edu/science/key-concepts/resilience/

Chapter 22
A Kid-First Co-Parenting Plan

A simple template to turn good intentions into a stable week

Plans protect children when emotions run hot
When families are under stress, the problem is not that adults don't care. The problem is that care without structure collapses under pressure.

A kid-first co-parenting plan is not a legal document. It is a stability document.

It answers the questions children silently ask every week:

Where will I be? Who will pick me up? What happens if someone cancels? How do my adults talk to each other? What are the rules that don't change?

When plans are clear, adults fight less and children settle faster.

Co-parenting research frameworks emphasize that coordination, reduced undermining, and clearer role functioning support child and family adjustment—especially in high-stress contexts.1

Family-court and clinical literatures also emphasize that parenting plans work best when they are developmentally appropriate, specific enough to reduce ambiguity, and structured to reduce conflict exposure.2

When conflict is high, structured supports such as parenting coordination (where available) may help implement child-centered plans and reduce repeated disputes.3

Reducing chronic stressors and uncertainty is also consistent with developmental science on buffering toxic stress through stability and supportive relationships.4

Step 1: Choose your lane (cordial, parallel, protective)

Before you write a plan, choose a lane. The lane determines how much coordination is realistic right now.

Cordial: You can talk and problem-solve respectfully.

Parallel: Minimal, structured communication.

Protective: Safety-focused boundaries; increased supervision/support.

Lane changes are allowed by season. A kid-first plan is flexible enough to adjust and clear enough to hold.

The Kid-First Plan Template (fill in the blanks)
Keep it to 1–2 pages. Short plans get used. Long plans get argued about.

Use these sections:

A) Weekly schedule: Where the child is each day, and exact exchange times/locations.

B) Transition rules: Brief, calm, child-centered handoffs; no discussions at the door.

C) Communication rules: One channel; response window; BIFF tone; emergencies defined.

D) The backup plan: What happens if someone cancels (by what time), and who covers.

E) Non-negotiables: 5 rules that hold across homes (safety, respect, routines).

F) School and activities: Who receives communication; who can pick up; fees and calendars.

G) Medical and safety: How urgent issues are communicated; medication routines; safe storage.

H) Conflict reset: How disputes are handled (24-hour pause; consult third party; return to kid-first filter).

I) Review rhythm: A monthly (cordial) or quarterly (parallel/protective) plan check-in date/time.

The backup plan is the child's emotional safety net

If you only build one part of a plan, build the backup plan.

Children become more stable when disappointment is not a surprise and chaos is not the default.

A kid-first backup plan answers:

• By what time does a caregiver confirm the visit?

• What happens if confirmation doesn't come?

• Who is the backup adult, and what is the alternate activity?

This is not punitive. It's predictable.

Example plan language (copy/paste)

Transition rule: "Exchanges will be brief and calm. No discussions at the door. Any concerns will be sent in writing within 24 hours."

Communication rule: "All non-urgent communication will occur by email. Response window: within 24 hours. Tone: brief and child-focused."

Confirmation rule: "Caregiver will confirm by 3:00 p.m. on the day of pickup. If not confirmed, the backup plan will be used."

In the next chapter: we'll focus on when the whole system lacks capacity—and keep translating kid-first values into daily, doable steps.

Backup plan: "If a visit cancels, the child will spend the evening with ___, and we will do ___ (predictable activity)."

Conflict reset: "We pause for 24 hours when possible, consult one neutral helper if stuck, and return to the Kid-First Filter."

Make it stick: If–Then plans
One reason plans fail is that stress wipes out memory. If–Then plans help because they pre-decide behavior: "If X happens, then we do Y."5

Write three If–Then lines:

- If a message is provocative, then I respond with BIFF or I wait 24 hours.

- If a visit is not confirmed by the deadline, then we use the backup plan without arguing.

A Small Step This Week
This week, build a one-page plan draft. Don't perfect it—start it.

- Choose your lane.

- Write the weekly schedule and transition rules.

- Write the backup plan (confirmation time + alternate coverage).

- Choose your five non-negotiables.

A one-page plan you use is better than a ten-page plan you fight about.

Closing prayer
God, help us build stability with wisdom and humility.

Give us clear plans that protect children from last-minute chaos.

Help us follow through with steadiness, even when emotions rise.

Let structure become a gift of peace, and let our home(s) be places where children can breathe.

Amen.

Kid-First takeaway: the win is a child who feels loved, safe, and protected—while adult problems stay in adult hands.

Chapter 22 Endnotes (APA 7th Edition)

1. Feinberg, M. E. (2003). The internal structure and ecological context of coparenting: A framework for research and intervention. Parenting: Science and Practice, 3(2), 95–131.

2. Saini, M., Drozd, L. M., & Olesen, N. W. (2017). Parenting plan evaluations: Applied research for the family court. Oxford University Press.

3. Association of Family and Conciliation Courts. (2019). Guidelines for parenting coordination. https://www.afccnet.org/Portals/0/Committees/Gu idelines%20for%20Parenting%20Coordination%20 2019.pdf

4. Center on the Developing Child at Harvard University. (n.d.). Toxic stress. https://developingchild.harvard.edu/science/key-concepts/toxic-stress/

5. Gollwitzer, P. M. (1999). Implementation intentions: Strong effects of simple plans. American Psychologist, 54(7), 493–503. https://doi.org/10.1037/0003-066X.54.7.493

Chapter 23
When the System
Lacks Capacity

Where does the child go when adults can't show up—and how to build safety without shame

Sometimes the problem isn't "co-parenting." It's "no stable parent."

Most co-parenting books assume there are two adults with enough capacity to show up consistently.

But many of the families you and I both serve don't have that. The caregivers are unstable, overwhelmed, ill, impaired, absent, or locked in constant conflict.

In those situations, the kid-first question gets painfully simple:

Where does the child go when the adults cannot show up?

This chapter is for the hardest cases—when the whole system lacks capacity—and you still want to act with dignity, wisdom, and urgency.

Child welfare guidance describes kinship care as relatives or trusted adults stepping in when parents cannot provide safe, consistent care—often as a preferred option when it can be stable and safe.1

Pediatric guidance also notes that kinship caregivers frequently need coordinated support (legal, financial, medical, respite) to sustain stability over time.2

Public health frameworks emphasize preventing and buffering adversity and toxic stress through safe environments, stable relationships, and supportive systems.346

What we mean by "capacity"
Capacity is not about worth. It is about ability.

A caregiver may love a child deeply and still be unable to provide consistent safety, supervision, and emotional steadiness.

Capacity includes:

- Safety: the ability to protect the child from harm (including safe supervision).

- Consistency: the ability to keep basic routines and follow through on plans.

- Regulation: the ability to stay emotionally steady enough that the child is not living in fear.

- Functioning: the ability to handle basic needs— school, meals, hygiene, medical care.

Kid-first love tells the truth about capacity because children pay the price when adults pretend.

Kid-first triage: three levels of urgency
When the whole system is shaky, sort the situation into one of three levels:

Level 1: Strained but safe — Adults are inconsistent, but the child is safe and supervised. The need is structure, support, and a village plan.

A Note for Grandparents and Kinship Caregivers
If you are raising a child you did not expect to raise, you may feel two things at once: fierce love and fierce resentment. You can acknowledge the cost without shaming the child or dishonoring the parent in front of them. Your steadiness becomes the child's nervous system scaffold.

- Clarify roles: Who makes medical, school, and discipline decisions? Put it in writing when possible so the child isn't caught between adults.

- Create a simple house rhythm: mealtimes, bedtime, and school routines matter more than perfect parenting philosophies.

- Protect the child from adult commentary: process anger with another adult, counselor, or pastor—not in the child's hearing.

- Practice honor-with-truth: "Your mom loves you, and she's having a hard season. Our job is to keep you safe and steady."

Level 2: Unstable and risky — Supervision is unreliable, conflict is constant, routines collapse. The need is increased oversight, written plans, and professional involvement.

Level 3: Unsafe — There is credible risk of harm, neglect, violence, or severe impairment. The need is protective action and immediate support from appropriate authorities/professionals.

This chapter cannot replace local guidance. But it can help you think clearly, especially when everyone around you is reactive.

If it's strained but safe: build a coverage plan
When adults are strained but the child is safe, your first goal is coverage: making sure the child is never the one "falling through the cracks."

Use the Village chapter and add one more tool: the Coverage Map.

The Coverage Map answers one question: who is responsible for the child at every point in the week?

Coverage Map (write it down):

- Primary caregiver(s): who is responsible most days.

- Backup caregiver(s): who covers when the primary cannot.

- Emergency caregiver(s): who is available same-day in a crisis.

- Neutral exchange plan: where and how handoffs happen without adult conflict.

- Non-negotiables: school attendance, sleep routine, safe supervision.

A written coverage plan reduces arguments because it replaces "who wants to" with "what we already decided."

If it's unstable and risky: add structure + professional eyes

When the system is unstable and risky, the child may not be in immediate danger every day, but chronic unpredictability is shaping their nervous system.

In these seasons, kid-first care adds two things:

• tighter structure (less improvising),

• professional support (more eyes, more accountability).

Developmental science describes how chronic, unsupported stress can become toxic stress— especially when children lack stable, protective relationships.4

Kid-first structure in Level 2 often includes:

- One communication lane (parallel or protective).

- Written-only logistics and a response window.

- Neutral transitions or third-party exchange support.

- A clear cancellation/backup plan.

- Regular check-ins with school counselors or child providers when appropriate.

Trauma-informed guidance emphasizes safety, trust, collaboration, empowerment, and consistent routines—helpful anchors for children living in unpredictable systems.5

If it's unsafe: protective action is love
If you believe a child is unsafe, kid-first care does not tell you to "stay positive." It tells you to protect.

That may mean emergency services. It may mean child protective systems in your area. It may mean medical evaluation, supervised contact, or immediate placement with a safer caregiver.

If you are a pastor, mentor, or extended family member: do not try to privately manage what requires protection. Do not delay because you fear conflict. Children cannot afford our denial.

If you are a caregiver: you are not betraying someone by protecting a child. You are honoring what is sacred.

Public health guidance on preventing adverse childhood experiences emphasizes the importance of safe, stable, nurturing relationships and environments as key protective factors.[3]

So where does the child go?
Kid-first answers are not always neat. But they are clear:

The child goes to the safest stable environment available—where supervision, routines, and emotional steadiness are most likely to be sustained.

In practice, this often looks like one of these pathways:

- Stable kinship care: a grandparent, aunt/uncle, or trusted adult who can provide consistent care.

- Shared village care: a small coordinated team with clear roles (only when one stable "anchor" adult exists).

- Formal systems support: foster care/guardianship/other legal structures when no safe stable adult is available.

The kid-first question is not "Who deserves the child?" It is "Who can keep the child safe and steady right now?"

How to speak about low capacity without shame
When the system lacks capacity, the temptation is either to villainize or to romanticize.

Kid-first care does neither. It names reality with dignity.

Try this language:

To professionals: "We are concerned about stability and supervision. The child's routines are not being maintained consistently. We need a plan that prioritizes safety."

To extended family: "We're choosing the safest stable plan available. We're not debating adult blame in front of the child."

To a child (age-appropriate): "Some grown-ups are not able to take care of kids consistently right now.

That is not your fault. Your job is to be a kid. Our job is to keep you safe."

To the struggling caregiver (honor + boundary): "I care about you and I'm praying for you. Right now the child needs consistent safety, so the plan is ___. We can revisit as stability improves."

Next: we'll focus on for pastors, therapists, and helpers—and keep translating kid-first values into daily, doable steps.

For the one who keeps picking up the pieces
If you are the one who keeps stepping in, your anger may be real and understandable.

But bitterness is heavy, and children can feel its weight even when you never speak it.

Kid-first wisdom is not "don't feel angry." It is: feel it in adult places, and protect the child from it.

Ask yourself:

• What adult support do I need so I don't leak resentment onto the child?

• What respite do I need so my body can keep doing this with steadiness?

• What boundaries keep me from becoming the only functioning adult forever?

When caregivers are supported, children are protected. A village is not optional in low-capacity systems.

A Small Step This Week
If you are in a low-capacity system, do three things this week:

- Write a Coverage Map (primary, backup, emergency) and share it with the core adults.

- Choose your lane (parallel or protective is often necessary) and move logistics to one written channel.

- Schedule one professional consult (pediatric, therapy, school counselor, social services, or pastoral care) so you are not carrying this alone.

Kid-first care is not heroic solo parenting. It is organized love.

Closing prayer
God, have mercy on children living in unstable systems.

Give us courage to tell the truth about capacity without shame or cruelty.

Lead us to the safest stable plan, and surround this child with steady love.

Strengthen the caregivers who are stepping in, and open doors to the support we need.

Let protection be an act of honor, and let stability become a refuge.

Amen.

Kid-First takeaway: plan for reality, not ideals. Capacity can change, but children need steadiness today.

Chapter 23 Endnotes (APA 7th Edition)

1. Child Welfare Information Gateway. (n.d.). Kinship care. U.S. Department of Health and Human Services, Administration for Children and Families, Children's Bureau. https://www.childwelfare.gov/topics/permanency/kinship-care/

2. Rubin, D., Springer, S. H., Zlotnik, S., Kang-Yi, C. D., & Council on Foster Care, Adoption, and Kinship Care. (2017). Needs of kinship care families and pediatric practice. Pediatrics, 139(4), e20170099. https://doi.org/10.1542/peds.2017-0099

3. Centers for Disease Control and Prevention. (n.d.). Preventing adverse childhood experiences (ACEs). https://www.cdc.gov/violenceprevention/aces/

4. Center on the Developing Child at Harvard University. (n.d.). Toxic stress. https://developingchild.harvard.edu/science/key-concepts/toxic-stress/

5. Substance Abuse and Mental Health Services Administration. (2014). SAMHSA's concept of trauma and guidance for a trauma-informed approach (HHS Publication No. SMA14-4884). https://store.samhsa.gov/product/SMA14-4884

6. World Health Organization. (2020). INSPIRE: Seven strategies for ending violence against children. https://www.who.int/publications/i/item/9789240021024

Chapter 24
For Pastors, Therapists, and Helpers

How to support kid-first families with clarity, boundaries, and hope

Helpers shape the atmosphere around a child

This book is written for caregivers, but many of the people who will recommend it are helpers: pastors, therapists, school staff, mentors, ministry leaders, and friends who keep stepping in.

If that is you, thank you for being a steady presence in complicated stories.

Children are shaped not only by their parents, but by the adults who surround them. Helpers can become stabilizers—or unintentionally become accelerators of conflict.

This chapter gives you a kid-first posture and a few practical boundaries so your support stays protective.

Start with scope: what is your role here?

One of the most common ways helpers get pulled into harm is role confusion.

A pastor becomes a therapist. A therapist becomes a judge. A mentor becomes an investigator. A friend becomes a legal strategist.

Kid-first care begins with clarity:

What is my role? What is not my role?

Scope protects children because it keeps support clean.

Professional ethical codes emphasize boundaries, competence, informed consent, and avoiding dual relationships that impair objectivity or increase harm.123

Pastoral care has its own ethical boundaries as well. Even when you can offer deep spiritual guidance, it is still wise to know where you refer and where you collaborate.

The kid-first helper posture: compassion plus structure

In complicated families, compassion alone is not enough. Compassion without structure often enables chaos.

Structure alone is not enough either. Structure without compassion creates shame and resistance.

Kid-first helpers learn to hold both: warm presence and clear boundaries.

Here are four posture commitments:

- Child-centered: I keep the child's stability, safety, and development in view.

- Non-triangulating: I do not become the messenger or the court of appeal between adults.

- Non-escalating: I do not inflame conflict with gossip, "taking sides," or public commentary.

- Skill-building: I help adults build regulation, communication, and routine—not just vent.

Trauma-informed support without trauma-driven decisions

Trauma-informed guidance emphasizes safety, trustworthiness, collaboration, empowerment, and cultural responsiveness—useful anchors for helper posture.4

But here is the balance: being trauma-informed does not mean being trauma-driven.

Trauma-driven decisions are reactive: made in panic, in anger, or in rescuing urgency without a plan.

Trauma-informed decisions are steady: they slow down when possible, name reality clearly, and build a structure that protects the child.

In the room: what to prioritize

Whether you are meeting with one caregiver or multiple adults, kid-first priorities look like this:

- Stabilize: begin with regulation (breath, prayer, grounding) so the meeting is not run by activation.

- Clarify: what is the child experiencing right now? What does the week look like for the child?

- Plan: what is the smallest stable plan we can implement in the next 7 days?

- Boundary: what will we keep out of the child's world (adult conflict, oversharing, loyalty pressure)?

- Support: who is on the child's team (school, therapy, medical, church, kinship supports)?

Church and Culture: Protecting the Child's Story

In some families and cultures, loyalty and privacy are sacred. That can be beautiful—until it becomes silence that leaves a child unprotected. Kid-first care holds confidentiality with wisdom: we don't spread stories, and we don't hide harm.

- Avoid public processing: don't turn a child's situation into a "prayer update" in a way that exposes them or fuels gossip.

- Choose language that honors without denial: "We're walking through a hard season and focusing on the child's stability."

- Don't recruit allies: church care should reduce triangulation, not amplify it.

- When safety is uncertain, involve appropriate local professionals and keep the focus on protection and steadiness.

Do not become a weapon

High-conflict systems often recruit helpers: "Tell them they're wrong." "Write a letter proving I'm right." "Take my side." "Confront the other parent."

Kid-first helpers refuse to become weapons.

You can be supportive without being weaponized.

You can say:

To a caregiver who wants you to attack the other adult: "I'm here to support stability for the child. I'm not going to escalate conflict, but I will help you build a plan and stay regulated."

When asked for a 'character letter' in a heated conflict: "I can describe what I have directly observed and how I've supported the child, but I won't make judgments about the other adult."

239

When someone wants you to carry messages: "I'm not a messenger. Please communicate directly through your agreed channel."

Documentation: facts only, observed only
If you are ever asked to document concerns, stick to what you observed:

• dates, times, behaviors, quotes (if appropriate), and observable impact on the child.

Avoid interpreting motives. Avoid diagnosing. Avoid repeating hearsay as fact.

These notes are for clarity and child safety—often to share with medical, school, counseling, or support teams—not to interrogate a child or to build a case.

Clear documentation protects children and protects helpers.

Safety concerns: act with urgency and appropriate referral
If you become aware of credible safety concerns, do not handle it privately out of fear of conflict.

Follow the local policies and safety procedures that apply to your role, and connect the family with appropriate professionals who can assess risk and next steps.

If you are a pastor, counselor, teacher, or group leader, follow your local policies and legal/ethical requirements regarding child safety.

A helper's collaboration map

When things are complicated, map the supports and keep the lanes clear:

- Pastor/mentor: spiritual support, moral framing, accountability, prayer, community connection.

- Therapist/counselor: clinical assessment, skill-building, trauma treatment, family systems work.

- School team: daily observation, routine support, accommodations when stress impacts learning.

- Medical providers: injury evaluation, health screening, sleep and somatic complaints, referrals.

- Systems supports: legal counsel, parenting coordination, casework—when applicable.

In high-conflict contexts, structured supports like parenting coordination (where available) are described in professional guidelines as one approach to help implement child-focused plans and reduce repeated disputes.5

A Small Step This Week (for Helpers)

If you are supporting a complicated family right now, do three things this week:

- Clarify your role in one sentence and communicate it ("I'm here for child stability and adult skill-building").

- Help the caregiver build one 7-day plan (coverage, routines, communication lane).

- Identify one referral or collaboration step (school counselor, therapy consult, medical evaluation, parenting coordination, etc.).

Helpers multiply hope when they reduce chaos and increase clarity.

Closing prayer

God, make me a wise helper in complicated stories.

Give me compassion that is steady and structure that is kind.

Protect me from being pulled into triangulation, gossip, or conflict escalation.

Help me advocate for children with courage, and refer with humility when needs exceed my role.

Let my presence bring peace and clarity—so children can grow in safety and love.

Amen.

Kid-First takeaway: the win is a child who feels loved, safe, and protected—while adult problems stay in adult hands.

Chapter 24 Endnotes (APA 7th Edition)

1. American Psychological Association. (2017). Ethical principles of psychologists and code of conduct (2002, amended 2010, 2017). https://www.apa.org/ethics/code

2. American Counseling Association. (2014). ACA code of ethics. https://www.counseling.org/resources/aca-code-of-ethics

3. American Association for Marriage and Family Therapy. (2015). Code of ethics. https://www.aamft.org/Legal_Ethics/Code_of_Ethics.aspx

4. Substance Abuse and Mental Health Services Administration. (2014). SAMHSA's concept of trauma and guidance for a trauma-informed approach (HHS Publication No. SMA14-4884). https://store.samhsa.gov/product/SMA14-4884

5. Association of Family and Conciliation Courts. (2019). Guidelines for parenting coordination. https://www.afccnet.org/Portals/0/Committees/Gu

idelines%20for%20Parenting%20Coordination%20
2019.pdf

6. Christian, C. W.; Committee on Child Abuse and Neglect. (2015). The evaluation of suspected child physical abuse. Pediatrics, 135(5), e1337–e1354. https://doi.org/10.1542/peds.2015-0356

In the pages ahead: we'll focus on keep the main thing the main thing—and keep translating kid-first values into daily, doable steps.

If you are a friend or family member, you can still help: stay calm, write down what you observed (facts only), and connect the caregiver with local professionals and child-safety resources.

Clinical guidance emphasizes that suspected child physical abuse should be evaluated carefully and systematically by appropriate professionals.6

Chapter 25
Keep the Main Thing the Main Thing

A closing charge for kid-first families—and a steady way forward

This is not about perfect adults. It's about protected children.

If you have made it to the end of this book, you have done something many people never do: you have faced reality and chosen growth.

Kid-first co-parenting is not a strategy to make adults feel better about each other. It is a commitment to make childhood safer—especially when adult relationships are complicated.

And yes, it is work.

It is the work of pausing when you want to react, repairing when you miss it, and choosing structure when your emotions want control.

But the fruit is worth it: children who can breathe, trust, and grow.

The kid-first anchors (a short recap)

When you feel overwhelmed, return to these anchors:

- Safety: Protect the child's body, mind, and spirit.
- Stability: Build routines and predictability so the child can count on life.
- Respect: Keep children out of adult conflict and loyalty pressure.
- Regulation: Steady adults create steadier children.
- Repair: When things break, return to love and rebuild trust over time.

Resilience research consistently shows that children can do well even after adversity when protective factors are present—especially stable relationships, supportive environments, and skill-building over time.13

Co-parenting intervention research likewise suggests that improving the quality of co-parenting and reducing undermining can benefit children's adjustment.2

In plain language: kids don't need a perfect story. They need enough steady love to grow strong.

When you feel like quitting
What we'll tackle next: you'll find practical appendices—scripts, checklists, and templates you can use immediately to support stability.

There will be days you want to give up on cooperation. Days you are tired of being the mature one. Days you are angry at someone else's lack of capacity.

On those days, remember: kid-first maturity is not agreement. It is leadership.

Leadership is doing the next right thing even when someone else doesn't.

If you are the only steady adult in the system right now, your steadiness matters more than you know.

A weekly rhythm that keeps you grounded
If you want a simple practice to keep kid-first alive, try this weekly rhythm:

- Sunday (or your reset day): Look at the week schedule. Confirm transitions. Review the backup plan.

- Midweek: One 10-minute check-in (with a co-parent, or with your village) to prevent chaos.

- Daily: One regulation habit (prayer, walk, breath, journaling) so your child isn't carrying your stress.

- As needed: Repair within 24 hours when conflict or sharpness shows up.

Practices like emotion coaching and whole-brain approaches emphasize naming feelings, building regulation through connection, and returning to repair—skills that strengthen children over time.45

Your child will remember how safe they felt
One day your child will not remember every schedule change or every difficult conversation.

But they will remember the atmosphere.

They will remember whether adults could return to calm.

They will remember whether they had permission to be a child.

They will remember if love was steady—even when life was not.

Final prayer and blessing
Put simply: God, help us keep the main thing the main thing.

Protect the children in complicated stories from carrying what adults have not resolved.

Give caregivers wisdom, humility, and strength to build stability—one steady step at a time.

Heal what has been wounded. Restore what has been fractured. Redeem what feels impossible.

Let our homes be refuges of peace, and let our children grow up knowing they are safe, seen, and deeply loved.

Amen.

Kid-First takeaway: the win is a child who feels loved, safe, and protected—while adult problems stay in adult hands.

Chapter 25 Endnotes (APA 7th Edition)

1. Masten, A. S. (2014). Ordinary magic: Resilience in development. Guilford Press.

2. Sandler, I. N., Wolchik, S. A., Winslow, E., Mahrer, N. E., Moran, J. A., Weinstock, D., & Schenck, C. (2012). Quality of coparenting and child adjustment after divorce: A randomized trial. Journal of Consulting and Clinical Psychology, 80(4), 706–717.

3. Center on the Developing Child at Harvard University. (n.d.). Resilience. https://developingchild.harvard.edu/science/key-concepts/resilience/

4. Gottman, J., & DeClaire, J. (1997). Raising an emotionally intelligent child. Simon & Schuster.

5. Siegel, D. J., & Bryson, T. P. (2011). The Whole-Brain Child: 12 revolutionary strategies to nurture your child's developing mind. Bantam.

APPENDIX A

Kid-First Decision Framework

The Main Thing
The main thing is building a stable, loving environment where children can thrive—no matter how complicated the family structure becomes. When adults stay grounded and intentional, children can grow with greater peace, security, and confidence—even in imperfect and painful circumstances.

A note about honoring an unwell parent
There are seasons when a parent, due to illness, addiction, or mental health struggles, is unable to fulfill the role of parenting in a consistent way. This framework helps you accomplish the main thing while still honoring that parent with dignity and compassion. Honoring someone does not mean ignoring reality or sacrificing safety. It means telling the truth with love, setting wise boundaries, and creating stability where it is possible.

Before you decide: Pause and name the moment
When tension rises, decisions get rushed. Use this 30–60 second pause before texting, reacting, or making changes:

- What is happening right now (fact, not interpretation)?

- What is the child experiencing because of this?

- What am I feeling—and what am I afraid will happen?

- What decision would build stability and reduce chaos?

Kid-First Filter: The 7 Questions

Run any decision through these questions. If you can't answer a question clearly, slow down and get help.

- Safety: Does this protect the child physically, emotionally, and spiritually?

- Stability: Will this reduce disruption and increase predictability (routines, schedules, expectations)?

- Belonging: Does this help the child feel loved and secure in both homes (or in the home they live in)?

- Respect: Does this avoid putting the child in the middle or asking them to carry adult messages?

- Development: Is this age-appropriate, and does it support the child's long-term growth?

- Peace: Will this lower conflict exposure for the child (even if it doesn't make adults happy)?

- Legacy: Will this decision help build a story the child can be proud of later?

Honor-with-Boundaries Check (when a parent is unwell)
Use this section when illness, addiction, or instability affects parenting. It helps you hold compassion and clarity at the same time.

- Honor: Can I speak about the parent with dignity, without covering harm or pretending things are okay?

- Truth: Am I naming reality clearly (to myself, to my spouse, and when needed, to professionals)?

- Access: What level of contact is healthy right now—full, supervised, limited, or paused?

- Consistency: Am I protecting routines and emotional steadiness for the child?

- Support: Who needs to be involved (counselor, pastor, sponsor, medical care, legal support) to keep the child safe?

Choose a pathway: Cordial, Parallel, or Protective

Not every family can co-parent the same way in every season. Choose the healthiest pathway for the child right now:

Cordial Co-Parenting: Communication is respectful. You can coordinate calendars, discuss needs, and problem-solve together.

Parallel Parenting: Communication is minimal and structured. Each home runs its routine with clear boundaries to reduce conflict exposure for the child.

Protective Parenting: When safety is at risk, you tighten boundaries and increase supervision/support. You prioritize safety and stability over togetherness.

Simple scripts (use, don't over-explain)

To the other parent (cordial): "For the child's sake, I'd like us to keep this calm and clear. Here's what I'm proposing…"

To the other parent (parallel): "I'm going to keep communication brief and focused on logistics. Please send updates by text/email."

When the parent is unwell: "I care about you, and I'm praying for your health. Right now we need consistency and safety for the child, so we're going to…"

To a child (age-appropriate): "Both of your parents love you. Sometimes adults have struggles that make things complicated. Our job is to keep you safe and cared for."

To extended family: "We're making decisions based on the child's stability and well-being. We appreciate support, not pressure."

Closing prayer (first person)
God, help me keep the main thing the main thing. Give me wisdom to build stability and love for these children, even when the adults are strained, wounded, or divided. Teach me to honor people with dignity while also telling the truth and setting boundaries that protect what is sacred. Give me courage to choose peace over power, and faith to believe that steady love can shape a legacy—even in a complicated story. Amen.

APPENDIX B

Transition Toolkit

Neurodiversity Notes (ADHD, Autism, Sensory Sensitivity)

Some children struggle with transitions not because they are oppositional, but because shifting gears is neurologically hard. When in doubt, add structure and reduce sensory load.

- Use visual supports: a simple picture checklist for packing, arrival, and bedtime.

- Give time warnings: "10 minutes, then shoes." "2 minutes, then car."

- Build a sensory buffer: headphones, a fidget, a quiet corner, a weighted blanket, or a short walk after arrival.

- Keep instructions short: one step at a time. Praise effort, not speed.

- If meds, therapy, or school supports exist, keep both homes aligned on thc basics (timing, expectations) when possible.

Home changes are one of the most common places children dysregulate—especially in complicated systems. Transitions can stir grief, loyalty pressure, sensory overload, and fear of what mood they're walking into. This toolkit gives you simple, repeatable practices so the child's nervous system experiences change as predictable—not chaotic.

The goal of a kid-first transition

A kid-first transition is not a performance of adult cooperation. It is a regulated handoff that protects the child from adult intensity. The goal is simple: short, calm, predictable, and child-centered.

The four rules of kid-first transitions

- Keep the doorway clean: no conflict, no processing, no debates at handoff.

- Keep it brief: the longer it lasts, the more likely it escalates.

- Keep the child out of adult messages: no "tell your mom/dad…"

- Keep the first ten minutes predictable: connection + settle + routine.

Before the transition (the day before + the hour before)

Use the same rhythm every time. Consistency is calming.

- Confirm logistics in writing (time, location, who is transporting).

- Pack with the child if age-appropriate (it reduces anxiety and builds control).

- Preview the plan: "Today is a change day. Here's what happens first when we get there."

- Lower stimulation: avoid rushing, extra errands, or emotionally heavy conversations right before handoff.

- Do one regulation practice (breathing, short walk, prayer) so you don't bring activation to the doorway.

At the exchange (1–3 minutes)
Think "airport drop-off," not "relationship meeting."

- Use a neutral tone and neutral words.

- Limit conversation to immediate child logistics (medicine, school item, pickup note).

- If tension rises, end the exchange: "Thanks. Have a good day." Follow up in writing later.

- If safety is a concern, use neutral locations, third-party exchanges, or supervised support as needed.

Simple doorway scripts
Cordial: "Hi. Here's the backpack. Pickup is Sunday at 5:00. Thanks."

Parallel: "Hi. Backpack is here. Please send updates by text/email."

When provoked: "I'm going to keep this focused on the child. We can follow up in writing."

When you need to leave quickly: "We're going to head out now. Thank you."

The first ten minutes after the child arrives (the Settle Routine)
Many children melt down after transitions not because the other home was "bad," but because their nervous system is finally safe enough to release.

Try this 10-minute routine:

1) Connect: eye contact, warmth, a simple greeting, a hug if welcomed.

2) Regulate: snack/water, bathroom break, change clothes if helpful, quiet corner or movement.

3) Predict: "Here's what's next" (unpack, play, dinner, bath, bedtime).

If your child dysregulates after transition
Use the Regulation Ladder: body → feelings →
choices.

- Body: slow down, offer water/snack, change
  environment, movement, grounding.

- Feelings: "I see you're _____. It makes sense—
  change days are hard."

- Choices: "You may _____ (safe option). I won't
  let you _____ (unsafe behavior)."

- Repair: "That was big. You're still loved. We're
  learning what to do with big feelings."

Do not interrogate (a kid-first debrief)
After visits, adults often ask too many questions
because they want reassurance or proof. That can
pressure children and increase loyalty conflict.

Instead, use one open door and one boundary:

- Open door: "If you want to talk about anything
  from your time there, I'm here."

- Boundary: "You don't have to answer lots of
  questions. Your job is to be a kid."

The Two-Home Backpack checklist
A consistent packing routine lowers anxiety.
Adjust for age and needs.

- School items: homework folder, device/charger, library books.

- Comfort item: small blanket, stuffed animal, sensory item.

- Clothes: 1–2 extra outfits, pajamas, weather gear.

- Health: medications (if applicable), inhaler/epi pen plan, glasses/retainers.

- Routine items: toothbrush/hair care if not duplicated in both homes.

- Notes: any simple update that is child-centered (not emotional commentary).

Special transitions (holidays, long breaks, new seasons)

Bigger changes need more preview and more predictability.

- Preview early: talk about the schedule several days ahead (age-appropriate).

- Use visuals: calendar on the fridge, color-coding, countdown notes for younger kids.

- Expect more feelings: plan extra connection and earlier bedtime after long breaks.

- Don't stack stress: avoid major discipline conversations on the first day back.

- If the child returns activated, return to the Settle Routine before problem-solving.

A short prayer for change days

God, give us peace in the doorway and steadiness in the home. Help this child feel safe through change. Help me be regulated, kind, and clear. Let routines become comfort and love become steady. Amen.

APPENDIX C

Kid-First Scripts Library

When emotions run high, words disappear. This script library gives you ready language that is short, respectful, and child-centered. Use these scripts as written, or adapt them to your tone. The goal is not perfect wording—the goal is reducing conflict exposure for the child.

1) Scripts for co-parent communication (cordial lane)

Scheduling: "For the child's sake, I'd like to keep this calm and clear. Here's what I'm proposing: ___."

Clarifying a plan: "Just confirming: pickup is ___ at ___. Please reply YES to confirm."

A small request: "Can you please ___ by ___? That will help the child have predictability."

When you disagree: "I see it differently. Let's choose the option that lowers conflict exposure for the child."

2) Scripts for co-parent communication (parallel lane)

Setting the lane: "I'm going to keep communication brief and focused on logistics. Please send updates by text/email."

Response window: "I've received your message. I'll respond within 24 hours."

Ending a debate: "I'm not going to debate this. Here is the plan for today: ___."

Boundary on tone: "I will respond to child logistics. I won't respond to insults."

3) Scripts for high-conflict moments
When bait arrives: "I'm going to keep this focused on the child's logistics. Pickup remains ___."

When accusations come: "I'm not going to argue. Here's what I'm doing today for the child: ___."

When messages escalate: "I will respond to child logistics only. If this continues, I will pause and respond later."

When you need to disengage: "I'm ending this conversation now. We can follow up in writing."

4) Scripts when a caregiver is unwell (honor + boundary)
Honor + plan: "I care about you, and I'm praying for your health. Right now the child needs consistency and safety, so we're going to ___."

Naming reality (adult-to-adult): "Here are the facts I'm seeing over time: ___. I'm making plans based on stability for the child."

Access boundary: "For now, contact will be ___ (supervised/limited/paused) so the child stays safe and regulated."

Revisit later: "We can revisit access as stability improves. My priority is the child's predictability."

5) Scripts for children (age-appropriate, no diagnosis)

Not your fault: "This is not your fault. Adults are responsible for adult choices."

Two truths: "You can enjoy the good moments, and you can still be safe when things are hard."

Big feelings: "You're not in trouble for having feelings. We're learning what to do with them."

When a visit cancels: "I'm sorry. I know that hurts. It's not your fault. We have a plan for today, and you are safe."

Loyalty pressure: "You don't have to choose sides. You're allowed to love the people you love."

Worry about an adult: "It's kind that you care. Adults are responsible for adult choices. Your job is to be a kid."

6) Scripts for extended family and the village

Setting boundaries: "We're making decisions based on the child's stability and well-being. We appreciate support, not pressure."

Stopping gossip: "We can talk privately. In front of the child, we keep it respectful and steady."

When people push sides: "I'm not debating adult blame. I'm building stability for the child."

Asking for help: "Can you help with ___ on ___ day for the next ___ weeks? It would really support consistency."

7) Scripts for schools, counselors, and professionals

Email to school: "Our family has transitions on ___. You may notice big feelings after change days. What helps is a brief check-in and predictable routine. Please send communication to ___."

To a therapist: "Our goal is stability and regulation for the child. Can we focus on transition coping tools and routines?"

When asked for details: "I'm keeping adult details private. What matters is supporting the child's stability."

A final reminder

Scripts are not magic words. They are boundaries in sentence form. When you keep your words short, calm, and child-centered, you lower the temperature—and your child gets to breathe.

APPENDIX D

Emotion Regulation Tools for Adults

You can't give children peace if your nervous system is constantly on fire. This appendix is for the caregiver who is trying to stay kind, wise, and steady—especially when someone else is not. These tools are simple on purpose. Complexity is hard to use when you are activated.

The goal: regulated leadership

Regulated leadership means you can feel anger, fear, grief, or frustration without letting those emotions drive your decisions. You are not trying to be emotionless. You are trying to be steady. Children do not need a perfect adult. They need an adult who can return to calm and keep the main thing the main thing.

1) The 60-second reset (anywhere, anytime)

Use this when you feel your body surge (rage-texting, panic, spiraling thoughts):

- Name it: "My body is activated."

- Breathe: inhale for 4, exhale for 6 (repeat 6 times).

- Ground: feel your feet, relax your jaw, drop your shoulders.

- Choose: "I will not respond until I'm steady."

2) The 'I am the thermostat' prayer

Sometimes you need words that turn down the temperature. Try this breath prayer:

Inhale: "Lord, make me steady."

Exhale: "Let peace lead me."

3) The JADE stop (when you want to justify, argue, defend, explain)

If you are co-parenting with someone who escalates, JADE is gasoline. Use this quick rule:

If I'm explaining to be understood, I'm in danger. If I'm stating logistics, I'm safe.

Replace JADE with one BIFF sentence:

BIFF = Brief, Informative, Friendly, Firm (one topic, one request, no bait-taking).

"Here is the plan for the child: ___. Please confirm."

4) The anger-to-action translation

Anger often contains a value. It is your nervous system saying, "Something sacred is being threatened." Translate anger into a wise action instead of a sharp reaction.

Ask:

- What value is my anger protecting? (safety, respect, fairness, stability)

- What boundary would protect that value without creating more chaos?

- What is the smallest next right step?

5) The 'adult places' rule

If you need to vent, vent in adult places—not to the child. Choose your adult outlet:

- A therapist or counselor

- A pastor or mentor

- A trusted friend who is steady and child-centered

- A journal (write it, don't text it)

- A support group (when appropriate)

6) The three-circle boundary (what I control / influence / release)

This tool reduces helplessness. Draw three circles and sort your stress:

- Control: my tone, my home routines, my boundaries, my follow-through.

- Influence: invitations, proposals, documentation, requesting support, professional consults.

- Release: the other adult's choices, personality, and capacity.

Spend 80% of your energy in the Control circle. Most burnout comes from fighting in the Release circle.

7) When you feel bitterness growing

Bitterness is what happens when grief and anger have nowhere to go. If you are the one holding everything together, bitterness is understandable— but it is also heavy for children to live near.

Try this three-step practice:

- Name the loss: "This is not what I wanted."

- Ask for help: "I need respite / support / coverage."

- Choose one act of honor: "In front of the child, I will speak with dignity and truth."

8) A short boundary script for your own mouth

When you are tempted to say something about the other caregiver in front of the child, pause and use this:

"I'm going to keep adult issues in adult places. You're safe with me."

A closing prayer
God, steady my nervous system when I feel pulled into chaos. Help me lead with wisdom and compassion. Guard my words so children are not carrying adult bitterness. Give me courage to set boundaries, humility to ask for help, and strength to keep doing the next right thing. Amen.

APPENDIX E

Recommended Reading and Resources (APA 7th Edition)

This book is designed to be practical and readable. If you want to go deeper—personally, clinically, or pastorally—these resources are widely used and respected. The list is intentionally curated (not exhaustive). Use it as a next step for your own growth, your counseling toolkit, or your church care team.

Co-Parenting, High-Conflict, and Family Systems

Eddy, B., Burns, A. T., & Chafin, K. (2020). BIFF for Coparent Communication: Your guide to difficult texts, emails, and social media posts. Unhooked Books/High Conflict Institute Press.

Saini, M., Drozd, L. M., & Olesen, N. W. (2017). Parenting plan evaluations: Applied research for the family court. Oxford University Press.

Feinberg, M. E. (2003). The internal structure and ecological context of coparenting: A framework for research and intervention. Parenting: Science and Practice, 3(2), 95–131.

Association of Family and Conciliation Courts. (2019). Guidelines for Parenting Coordination.

https://www.afccnet.org/Portals/0/Committees/Gu
idelines%20for%20Parenting%20Coordination%20
2019.pdf

Emotion Regulation and Emotion Coaching

Gottman, J., & DeClaire, J. (1997). Raising an
emotionally intelligent child. Simon & Schuster.

Siegel, D. J., & Bryson, T. P. (2011). The Whole-
Brain Child: 12 revolutionary strategies to nurture
your child's developing mind. Bantam.

Gross, J. J. (2015). Emotion regulation: Current
status and future prospects. Psychological Inquiry,
26(1), 1–26.
https://doi.org/10.1080/1047840X.2014.940781

Trauma, Attachment, and Resilience

van der Kolk, B. A. (2014). The body keeps the
score: Brain, mind, and body in the healing of
trauma. Viking.

Perry, B. D., & Szalavitz, M. (2006). The boy who
was raised as a dog: And other stories from a child
psychiatrist's notebook. Basic Books.

Johnson, S. M. (2019). Attachment theory in
practice: Emotionally focused therapy (EFT) with
individuals, couples, and families. Guilford Press.

Masten, A. S. (2014). Ordinary magic: Resilience in
development. Guilford Press.

Center on the Developing Child at Harvard University. (n.d.). Resilience. https://developingchild.harvard.edu/science/key-concepts/resilience/

Evidence-Based Support for Kids Under Stress
Cohen, J. A., Mannarino, A. P., & Deblinger, E. (2017). Trauma-focused CBT for children and adolescents: Treatment applications. Guilford Press.

American Academy of Pediatrics. (2018). Effective discipline to raise healthy children. Pediatrics, 142(6), e20183112. https://doi.org/10.1542/peds.2018-3112

Center on the Developing Child at Harvard University. (n.d.). Toxic stress. https://developingchild.harvard.edu/science/key-concepts/toxic-stress/

Kinship Care and 'The Village'
Child Welfare Information Gateway. (n.d.). Kinship care. U.S. Department of Health and Human Services, Administration for Children and Families, Children's Bureau. https://www.childwelfare.gov/topics/permanency/kinship-care/

Rubin, D., Springer, S. H., Zlotnik, S., Kang-Yi, C. D., & Council on Foster Care, Adoption, and

Kinship Care. (2017). Needs of kinship care families and pediatric practice. Pediatrics, 139(4), e20170099. https://doi.org/10.1542/peds.2017-0099

World Health Organization. (2020). INSPIRE: Seven strategies for ending violence against children. https://www.who.int/publications/i/item/97892400 21024

Safety, Abuse Evaluation, and Prevention
Christian, C. W.; Committee on Child Abuse and Neglect. (2015). The evaluation of suspected child physical abuse. Pediatrics, 135(5), e1337–e1354. https://doi.org/10.1542/peds.2015-0356

Centers for Disease Control and Prevention. (n.d.). Preventing child abuse and neglect. https://www.cdc.gov/violenceprevention/childabus eandneglect/

National Children's Alliance. (n.d.). Standards for accredited members. https://www.nationalchildrensalliance.org/

Faith-Informed Pastoral Support (wise boundaries + care)
Different traditions cite different pastoral counseling resources. The most important kid-first principle is this: use pastoral care to strengthen stability, accountability, and support—not to

intensify conflict or bypass safety. When needs exceed pastoral scope, collaborate and refer with humility.

How to use this list

- If you are a caregiver: choose one book that strengthens your regulation and one resource that strengthens your structure.

- If you are a pastor/mentor: keep one practical co-parenting resource and one trauma-informed resource on hand for referrals.

- If you are a therapist: consider pairing skill-building (regulation + routines) with coordination supports that reduce conflict exposure.

APPENDIX F

One-Page Kid-First Checklists
When families are stressed, the brain wants shortcuts. These checklists are designed to be printed or screenshotted. They bring you back to the main thing when you feel scattered.

1) The Weekly Stability Checklist
Use this once a week (5–10 minutes).

- Schedule confirmed (days/times/transport).

- Transitions protected (no conflict at the door; written follow-up later).

- Backup plan updated (who covers if plans fall through).

- Two routines protected (bedtime + one other rhythm).

- School communication set (who receives messages; pickup authorization).

- One adult support check-in scheduled (so the child isn't your outlet).

2) The Kid-First Decision Checklist (30–60 seconds)
Before you respond, decide, or react, ask:

- What's happening right now—what are the facts (not my interpretation)?

- What is my child experiencing in this moment because of what's happening?

- What decision builds stability and reduces chaos?

- Will my next step increase peace for the child— even if it costs my pride?

3) The Regulation Ladder (for meltdowns, transitions, big feelings)

Body → Feelings → Choices

- Body: slow down; snack/water; movement; change environment; grounding.

- Feelings: "I see ___. It makes sense because ___. We're safe."

- Choices: limit + skill + redo + repair.

4) The Clean Doorway Checklist (transitions)

- Brief (1–3 minutes).

- Neutral tone and words.

- No debates at the door.

- No adult messages through the child.

- First 10 minutes after arrival: connect + settle + predict.

5) The Village Map Checklist
Write names and numbers. Keep it updated.

- Ring 1 (Steady Care): who is consistently responsible?

- Ring 2 (Practical Support): who can help with pickups/meals/respite?

- Ring 3 (Professional Support): pediatrician, therapist, school counselor, pastor/mentor, legal/system supports as needed.

- One communication rule: adult conflict stays out of the child's hearing.

- One coverage rule: the child is never "up for grabs" day-to-day.

6) The One-Paragraph School Email Template
"Hello [Teacher/Counselor], I'm reaching out to support [Child's Name]. Our family has transitions on [days], and you may notice bigger feelings after change days. What helps is a brief check-in and predictable routine. Please send school communication to [name/email] and note that authorized pickup adults are [names]. Our goal is stability and low conflict exposure for [Child's Name]. Thank you for your support."

7) The Quick Repair Template

Use this when you miss it (to a child, or in your own heart):

- Name: "That was hard."

- Own: "I didn't handle that well."

- Protect: "That wasn't your job to carry."

- Plan: "Next time I will ___."

- Reconnect: "You are safe and loved."

Closing prayer

God, make me steady. Help me choose stability over winning, repair over pride, and peace over power. Keep the main thing the main thing, for the sake of these children. Amen.

APPENDIX G

Printable Kid-First Co-Parenting Plan Template

Use this template to create a simple, stable plan that reduces confusion and conflict exposure for children. Keep it to 1–2 pages. Short plans get used. Long plans get argued about.

A) Parenting lane (circle one)
☐ Cordial ☐ Parallel ☐ Protective

B) Weekly schedule (write it clearly)

Mon:
_____

Tue:
_____

Wed:
_____

Thu:
_____

Fri:
_____

Sat:
_____

Sun:
_____

C) Exchange details

Primary exchange location(s):

_____

Transport responsibility:

_____

Doorway rule (keep it clean): no conflict / no discussions / no messages through child.

D) Communication rules (choose one channel + response window)

Channel (circle one): Text Email App
Other: _____

Response window (circle one): Same day Within 24 hours Within 48 hours

Tone rule: brief, child-focused, no insults; logistics only when conflict is high.

E) The backup plan (the child's safety net)

Confirmation deadline (day/time):

_____

If not confirmed by the deadline, we will:

_____

Backup caregiver(s):

_____

Backup activity (predictable):

_____

F) Five non-negotiables (rules that hold across homes)

1)

_____

2)

_____

3)

_____

4)

_____

5)

_____

G) School and activities

School communication goes to:

_____

Authorized pickup adults:

_____

Activities schedule link/calendar:

_____

H) Health and safety

Medical provider(s):

_____

Medication/health routines (if applicable):

_____

Urgent issues will be communicated by (call/text):

_____

Emergency plan (who, where, what):

_____

I) Conflict reset (when we disagree)
☐ 24-hour pause when possible

☐ Consult one neutral helper
(pastor/counselor/mentor/professional)

☐ Return to the Kid-First Filter and choose the
decision that builds stability

J) Review date (when we revisit the plan)
Monthly / Quarterly review date:

_____

**Signatures (optional—this is a stability plan, not
legal advice)**
Caregiver 1: _____
Date: _____

Caregiver 2: _____
Date: _____

Other caregiver/guardian (if applicable):
_____ Date: _____

A short closing blessing

God, give us wisdom to build stability and humility to follow through. Help our words stay calm and our plans stay clear, so our child can breathe. Amen.

APPENDIX H

Frequently Asked Questions and Troubleshooting

Kid-first co-parenting looks simple on paper and complicated in real life. This appendix answers common questions in a way that keeps you grounded in what matters most: safety, stability, respect, regulation, and repair.

1) "My child melts down before or after transitions. What do I do?"

Assume stress before defiance. Many children fall apart at transitions because their nervous system is overloaded—or because they finally feel safe enough to release. Start with body-level support, then feelings, then choices.

Try this sequence:

- Body: snack/water, bathroom, movement, quiet space, predictable routine.

- Feelings: "Change days are hard. You're safe. I'm here."

- Choices: two safe options ("Do you want to unpack first or get a snack first?").

- Repair: if a meltdown turns into harsh words, return to connection after calm.

Do not interrogate your child about the other home during dysregulation. Settle first. Curiosity comes later, if needed.

2) "My child refuses to go to the other home."
Start by separating reluctance from risk. Some refusal is normal (separation anxiety, schedule change, loyalty pressure). But if a child reports fear, threats, violence, or unsafe supervision, take it seriously and seek appropriate professional guidance.

Kid-first steps:

- Validate without promising outcomes: "I hear you. I'm listening."

- Ask one open question: "What part feels hardest?" (avoid leading questions).

- Document facts (dates/times/what was said) without interrogating.

- Consult a child-centered professional (pediatric provider, therapist, school counselor) when concerns persist.

- If you believe safety is at risk, seek appropriate immediate support in your region.

3) "We have totally different rules in each home. Is that harming my child?"

Different homes will always feel different. The goal is not identical rules—it's shared non-negotiables. Choose 5 rules that hold across homes (safety, respect, sleep, school attendance, medication routines). Everything else can be flexible.

Use this line with your child:

"Different homes have different rhythms. What doesn't change is that you are safe and we treat each other with respect."

4) "The other parent cancels constantly. How do I stop my child from getting crushed?"

You cannot control another adult's follow-through, but you can control your child's predictability. Use a confirmation deadline and a backup plan every time.

Kid-first language for your child:

"I'm sorry. I know that's disappointing. It's not your fault. Here's our plan for today."

Over time, children stabilize when disappointment is met with compassion and a steady plan—not chaos and adult outrage.

5) "My co-parent sends long, angry messages. Should I respond?"

Respond to logistics, not provocation. Short, calm, and child-focused wins. If you are activated, wait. A delayed calm response is more protective than an immediate emotional one.

Try one BIFF response:

"Pickup remains 5:30. Please confirm YES. If not confirmed by 3:00, we'll use the backup plan."

6) "How do I introduce a new partner or blended family changes?"

Children need slow change, clear roles, and emotional safety. A new partner should not replace a parent role in the child's story; they should earn trust through steady presence over time.

Kid-first guidelines:

- Go slow: short, neutral interactions before big integration.

- Clarify roles: "This adult cares about you, but your parents remain your parents."

- Protect transitions: don't stack major changes on change days.

- Watch for loyalty pressure: reassure the child they don't have to choose sides.

7) "My teenager says they won't follow the schedule anymore."
Teens need more voice and more collaboration, but they still need structure and adult leadership. Start with curiosity: "What's not working?" Then problem-solve toward stability rather than abandoning structure.

Try this three-step conversation:

- Name: "I can see you're done with the current plan."

- Explore: "What's the hardest part—transition days, conflict, rules, relationships?"

- Negotiate: "Let's build a plan that keeps you safe and stable and gives you more voice."

8) "My family members criticize everything I do. How do I keep the village from becoming noise?"
Boundaries protect children. A child needs fewer steady adults, not many loud opinions. Use one sentence and repeat it—no over-explaining.

Boundary script:

"We're making decisions based on the child's stability and well-being. We appreciate support, not pressure."

9) "The child comes home dysregulated and says horrible things about the other home. What do I do?"

Start with regulation and containment. Children often vent big feelings in the safer home. You can empathize without fueling contempt or interrogating for details.

Try this response:

"That sounds like it was hard. I'm glad you told me. Let's get you settled first. If we need to talk more later, we will."

If safety concerns are named (harm, threats, injuries), document facts and seek appropriate professional support.

10) "What if I'm the one who keeps losing my temper?"

This is more common than people admit—especially when you are under chronic stress. Kid-first growth starts with honesty and a plan.

Three steps:

- Own it without shame: "I'm getting activated."

- Build a pause plan. "If I feel myself surging, I step away for 5 minutes."

- Get adult support: therapy, mentoring, pastoral care, or group support so your child isn't carrying your overflow.

11) "Do we have to agree on everything to be kid-first?"

No. Kid-first is not agreement. It is stability. Many families cannot coordinate deeply. They can still protect the child through parallel structure, clean transitions, and consistent routines.

12) "What's the simplest way to start if we're overwhelmed?"

Do three things for seven days:

- Protect the doorway (no conflict at transitions).

- Protect two routines (bedtime + one daily rhythm).

- Keep kids out of adult weight (no messages through the child; no venting to the child).

Small stability is not small. For a child's nervous system, it can be life-changing.

A final reminder

If you are carrying a high-risk situation (violence, credible threats, severe impairment, repeated injuries, unsafe supervision), this book is not a substitute for local professional and legal guidance.

Kid-first love protects children with both compassion and action.

Practical note: write down what you observed (facts only, not interpretations), keep communication calm and brief, and connect with local professionals who can help assess safety and next steps.

APPENDIX I

Safety and Support Resources

Some situations require more than wisdom and structure—they require immediate support. This appendix is not legal or medical advice. It is a quick reference to trusted resources.

If you believe a child may be harmed or is not safe, do not handle it alone. Contact local emergency services or a child advocacy/child protection hotline in your area, and seek professional support right away. When you are unsure, err on the side of the child's safety.

If you believe a child is in immediate danger

Call your local emergency number right away (in the U.S., 911). If you are unsure, err on the side of safety and consult local professionals.

U.S. national hotlines (24/7 unless noted)

Emergency: Call 911 (or your local emergency number).

Childhelp National Child Abuse Hotline: Call 1-800-4-A-CHILD (1-800-422-4453).

988 Suicide & Crisis Lifeline: Call or text 988, or use chat at 988lifeline.org.

Crisis Text Line: Text HOME to 741741 (U.S.).

National Domestic Violence Hotline: Call 1-800-799-SAFE (1-800-799-7233), or text START to 88788, or chat at thehotline.org.

love is respect (dating abuse support for teens/young adults): Call 866-331-9474 or text LOVEIS to 22522.

RAINN National Sexual Assault Hotline: Call 1-800-656-HOPE (1-800-656-4673), or use online chat via rainn.org.

National Human Trafficking Hotline: Call 1-888-373-7888 or text 233733 (BEFREE), or chat at humantraffickinghotline.org.

If you are outside the United States
Hotline numbers and services vary by country. If you are in immediate danger, contact your local emergency services. For verified international helplines, use these directories:

- International Association for Suicide Prevention (IASP) helplines directory: iasp.findahelpline.com

- Befrienders Worldwide helplines directory: befrienders.org

A note on digital safety
If you are in a high-control or abusive situation, your phone and browsing history may be

monitored. Consider using a trusted friend's device, a public computer, or a safer account when seeking help. Many hotlines offer web chat and safety planning for discreet access.

Appendix I References (APA 7th Edition)

Befrienders Worldwide. (n.d.). Befrienders Worldwide. https://befrienders.org/

Childhelp. (n.d.). National child abuse hotline. https://www.childhelp.org/hotline/

Crisis Text Line. (n.d.). Crisis Text Line. https://www.crisistextline.org/

International Association for Suicide Prevention. (n.d.). Find a helpline. https://iasp.findahelpline.com/

National Domestic Violence Hotline. (n.d.). Domestic violence support. https://www.thehotline.org/

National Human Trafficking Hotline. (n.d.). Contact us. https://humantraffickinghotline.org/en/contact

RAINN. (n.d.). National sexual assault hotline. https://rainn.org/help-and-healing/hotline/

Substance Abuse and Mental Health Services Administration. (n.d.). 988 Suicide & Crisis

Lifeline. https://www.samhsa.gov/mental-health/988

The Trevor Project. (n.d.). Here for you 24/7: How to reach out to The Trevor Project. https://www.thetrevorproject.org/resources/guide/here-for-you-24-7-how-to-reach-out-to-the-trevor-project/

APPENDIX J

Glossary of Kid-First Terms

This glossary keeps language consistent across the book. You can also use it as a quick reference when working with co-parents, caregivers, pastors, and professionals.

Attachment: A child's emotional bond with caregivers that shapes their sense of safety, trust, and regulation. Secure attachment grows through consistent care, protection, and repair.

BIFF communication: A message style designed to reduce escalation: Brief, Informative, Friendly, Firm. One topic. One request. No bait-taking.

Capacity: A caregiver's current ability (not worth) to provide safety, supervision, consistency, and emotional steadiness. Capacity can change by season.

Clean doorway: A transition practice: no conflict, no processing, and no debates at exchanges. The doorway is for the child, not adult power struggles.

Co-regulation: When a regulated adult helps a child regulate through presence, tone, rhythm, and connection. Over time, co-regulation builds the child's self-regulation.

Co-parenting: The shared work of caring for a child across two adults or two homes. Kid-first co-parenting prioritizes child stability and low conflict exposure.

Conflict exposure: The degree to which a child sees, hears, or senses adult conflict (including tense texting done in front of them). Lower exposure protects development.

Cordial co-parenting: A season where communication can be respectful and collaborative, allowing more coordination and problem-solving.

Coverage map: A written plan that answers: who is responsible for the child at every point in the week (primary, backup, emergency).

Dysregulation: A state where the nervous system is overwhelmed (fight/flight/freeze/shutdown). In dysregulation, logic is harder to access; the body needs settling first.

Emotion coaching: A parenting approach that names feelings, validates experience, teaches coping tools, and guides behavior with boundaries and repair.

Honor-with-boundaries: A posture that holds dignity and compassion for a struggling adult while still telling the truth and setting boundaries that protect the child.

JADE: A common escalation trap: Justify, Argue, Defend, Explain. In high-conflict systems, JADE often fuels more conflict.

Kid-first filter: A short set of questions used to guide decisions toward safety, stability, belonging, respect, development, peace, and legacy.

Legacy story: The long-term narrative a child carries about their family: what happened, what it meant, and whether love was steady.

Parallel parenting: A structure used when conflict is high: minimal, written, logistics-only communication, with clear boundaries so the child is not living inside adult conflict.

Protective parenting: A season where safety is at risk and boundaries tighten (supervision, limited contact, professional support). Safety and stability come first.

Repair: The practice of returning to love after a rupture: owning harm, naming impact, planning a new response, and reconnecting. Repair builds trust.

Rupture: A break in connection (yelling, sarcasm, withdrawal, intimidation, emotional shutdown).

Ruptures happen; the difference is whether adults repair.

Serve and return: A developmental concept describing responsive back-and-forth interaction: a child signals (serve) and a caregiver responds (return). Consistent return builds healthy brain circuitry.

Stability: Predictability in routines, schedules, expectations, and emotional climate—so a child can relax into life rather than brace for chaos.

Toxic stress: Chronic, severe stress without adequate adult buffering. Kid-first structure and supportive relationships help protect children by providing buffering and predictability.

Triangulation: Pulling a third person—often a child—into adult conflict (messages through the child, loyalty pressure, "take my side"). Kid-first care refuses triangulation.

Village: The circle of steady adults and supports around a child (kinship caregivers, mentors, teachers, providers). A kid-first village is organized with clear roles and boundaries.

Appendix J References (APA 7th Edition)
Center on the Developing Child at Harvard University. (n.d.). Serve and return interaction

shapes brain circuitry. https://developingchild.harvard.edu/science/key-concepts/serve-and-return/

Put simply: Center on the Developing Child at Harvard University. (n.d.). Toxic stress. https://developingchild.harvard.edu/science/key-concepts/toxic-stress/

Put simply: Eddy, B., Burns, A. T., & Chafin, K. (2020). BIFF for Coparent Communication: Your guide to difficult texts, emails, and social media posts. Unhooked Books/High Conflict Institute Press.

Put simply: Feinberg, M. E. (2003). The internal structure and ecological context of coparenting: A framework for research and intervention. Parenting: Science and Practice, 3(2), 95–131.

Put simply: Gottman, J., & DeClaire, J. (1997). Raising an emotionally intelligent child. Simon & Schuster.

Put simply: Siegel, D. J., & Bryson, T. P. (2011). The Whole-Brain Child: 12 revolutionary strategies to nurture your child's developing mind. Bantam.

APPENDIX K

Group Discussion Guide

A simple facilitator outline for churches, counseling centers, support groups, and caregiver teams

This book was written to be readable and usable. Many readers will also want a way to process it with others—a pastor's care team, a small group, a therapy group, a grandparent support circle, or a co-parenting class.

This guide is intentionally simple. It is not a curriculum that turns your healing into homework. It is a structure that protects the group from chaos and keeps the focus where it belongs: building child stability through adult steadiness.

Who this guide is for

- Church leaders and pastoral care teams offering support to single parents, blended families, kinship caregivers, and co-parents.

- Therapists or counselors running a psychoeducational group on co-parenting, regulation, and child stability.

- Grandparents and kinship caregivers needing a structured way to build a village and reduce conflict exposure.

- Mentors and helpers walking with complicated families who want shared language and tools.

Group ground rules (kid-first + trauma-aware)
Start every group with these boundaries. They protect participants and keep the focus on children, not drama.

- Confidentiality: what is shared here stays here—except when a child's safety is at risk.

- No diagnosing or labeling other people (especially not absent co-parents). We name the child's lived reality, not adult pathology.

- No legal strategy. This group is about stability and skills, not winning a case.

- No contempt talk in front of children—and no contempt talk here that trains you to speak with contempt later.

- Speak from "I": what I can control, what I can change, what I am learning.

- If a story includes safety concerns, we pause and make a plan to connect with appropriate professionals.

How to use the sessions
Recommended format: 60–90 minutes weekly for 6–8 weeks. Begin with a short regulation practice

(breath prayer or grounding), teach one concept, discuss in pairs or small groups, then end with one next step for the week.

Keep the rhythm steady. Consistency is regulating—especially for participants who live in chaos.

Six-session outline (recommended)

Session 1 — The Main Thing
- Key idea: Children should not carry what adults haven't resolved.

- Read/Discuss: the book's promise + Kid-First anchors.

- Practice: the 30–60 second pause (name the moment).

- Next step: identify one place your child is carrying adult stress—then remove one piece of that weight.

Session 2 — Regulation: becoming the steady adult
- Key idea: regulated adults create steadier children.

- Teach: what happens in the brain under stress (fight/flight/freeze) and why tone matters.

- Practice: the 60-second reset + one 'adult places' outlet plan.

- Next step: choose one regulation habit to do daily for 7 days.

Session 3 — Structure: routines, coverage, and the backup plan

- Key idea: structure is not cold; it's protective.

- Teach: the Coverage Map + two non-negotiable routines.

- Practice: build a one-week plan on paper.

- Next step: implement a confirmation deadline + backup plan for one recurring stress point.

Session 4 — Communication lanes: cordial, parallel, protective

- Key idea: not every family can co-parent the same way in every season.

- Teach: lane selection and BIFF messaging; why JADE escalates.

- Practice: rewrite one real message into BIFF.

- Next step: use one lane for 7 days without switching mid-conflict.

Session 5 — The village and the child's team

- Key idea: sometimes kid-first is not two parents—it's one circle.

- Teach: Circle of Care (Ring 1–3) + school/professional partnership.

- Practice: each participant names one helper role they need and writes one clear ask.

- Next step: make one specific ask for help (role + time + frequency).

Session 6 — The child's story: meaning, repair, and legacy

- Key idea: children grow up inside a story, and you influence what feels true.

- Teach: shame story vs contempt story vs resilience story; the power of repair.

- Practice: one repair script and one child-facing script ("not your fault").

- Next step: choose one story-building ritual (bedtime 'wins,' prayer, gratitude-with-truth).

Optional add-on sessions

- Transitions and two-home regulation: using the Transition Toolkit (Appendix B).

- High-conflict and safety boundaries: protective parenting without shame.

- Kinship caregiving and burnout: anger, grief, and staying honorable in front of kids.

Facilitator tips (pastoral + clinical)
- When someone escalates, slow the room down. Regulation is the first intervention.

- Keep bringing the group back to control vs influence vs release.

- Invite participants to name the child's experience in one sentence. Then plan the next right step.

- Watch for shame. Replace it with clarity: "This is hard. Here is what we can do."

- End every session with one small action. Stability grows through repetition, not inspiration alone.

Closing prayer for groups
God, help us keep the main thing the main thing. Make us steady adults for the sake of children. Give us wisdom to build structure, courage to set boundaries, and compassion that tells the truth with love. Heal what is wounded, strengthen what is fragile, and let peace grow in our homes. Amen.

Appendix K Endnotes (APA 7th Edition)

1. Sandler, I. N., Tein, J. Y., Wolchik, S., & Ayers, T. S. (2016). The effects of the New Beginnings Program on children and adolescents. Prevention Science, 17(1), 75–86.

2. Kazdin, A. E. (2005). Parent management training: Treatment for oppositional, aggressive, and antisocial behavior in children and adolescents. Oxford University Press.

3. Gollwitzer, P. M. (1999). Implementation intentions: Strong effects of simple plans. American Psychologist, 54(7), 493–503. https://doi.org/10.1037/0003-066X.54.7.493

APPENDIX L

Low-Capacity Quick Plan (Printable)
Use this page when you feel overwhelmed, impulsive, or emotionally flooded. Keep it on the fridge, in a notes app, or in a folder for helpers.

- Step 1 — Safety: Do I need backup care right now (supervision, a safe adult, a trusted family member, a childcare plan)? If yes, call now.

- Step 2 — Stability: What is the simplest plan I can keep today (meals, school, bedtime, medication, calm transition)?

- Step 3 — Communication lane: Keep contact brief and logistical. No processing by text. Pause if escalated.

- Step 4 — Repair: If I ruptured connection, I repair quickly: name it, apologize, reconnect.

Two scripts
To a helper/caregiver: "I'm not at my best today. For the child's stability, I need backup care from ___ to ___. I'll confirm by ___. Thank you."

To a child (age-appropriate): "I'm having a hard moment, and it's not your fault. I'm going to take a pause and get help so you stay safe and cared for. I love you."

Emergency note

If you believe a child is unsafe, follow local emergency procedures immediately (in the U.S., call 911). For additional resources, see Appendix I.

References

The references below consolidate major sources cited throughout the manuscript. Format: APA 7th Edition.

American Academy of Pediatrics. (2018). Effective discipline to raise healthy children. Pediatrics, 142(6), e20183112. https://doi.org/10.1542/peds.2018-3112

American Academy of Pediatrics. (n.d.). Bright Futures: Guidelines for health supervision of infants, children, and adolescents (selected guidance on psychosocial screening and family support). https://brightfutures.aap.org/

American Academy of Pediatrics. (n.d.). Media and children communication toolkit / family media plan. https://www.healthychildren.org/English/media/Pages/default.aspx

American Association for Marriage and Family Therapy. (2015). Code of ethics. https://www.aamft.org/Legal_Ethics/Code_of_Ethics.aspx

American Counseling Association. (2014). ACA code of ethics.

https://www.counseling.org/resources/aca-code-of-ethics

American Psychological Association. (2017). Ethical principles of psychologists and code of conduct (2002, amended 2010, 2017). https://www.apa.org/ethics/code

Arnsten, A. F. T. (2015). Stress weakens prefrontal networks: Molecular insults to higher cognition. Nature Neuroscience, 18, 1376–1385. https://doi.org/10.1038/nn.4087

Arnsten, A. F. T., Raskind, M. A., Taylor, F. B., & Connor, D. F. (2015). The effects of stress exposure on prefrontal cortex: Translating basic research into successful treatments for post-traumatic stress disorder. Neurobiology of Stress, 1, 89–99. https://doi.org/10.1016/j.ynstr.2014.10.002

Association of Family and Conciliation Courts. (2019). Guidelines for parenting coordination. https://www.afccnet.org/Portals/0/Committees/Guidelines%20for%20Parenting%20Coordination%202019.pdf

Befrienders Worldwide. (n.d.). Befrienders Worldwide. https://befrienders.org/

Bornstein, M. H., & Esposito, G. (2023). Coregulation: A multilevel approach via biology

and behavior. Children, 10(8), 1323.
https://doi.org/10.3390/children10081323

Boszormenyi-Nagy, I., & Spark, G. M. (1973).
Invisible loyalties: Reciprocity in intergenerational
family therapy. Harper & Row.

Center on the Developing Child at Harvard
University. (n.d.). Resilience.
https://developingchild.harvard.edu/science/key-concepts/resilience/

Center on the Developing Child at Harvard
University. (n.d.). Serve and return interaction
shapes brain circuitry.
https://developingchild.harvard.edu/science/key-concepts/serve-and-return/

Center on the Developing Child at Harvard
University. (n.d.). Toxic stress.
https://developingchild.harvard.edu/science/key-concepts/toxic-stress/

Centers for Disease Control and Prevention. (n.d.).
Preventing adverse childhood experiences (ACEs).
https://www.cdc.gov/violenceprevention/aces/

Centers for Disease Control and Prevention. (n.d.).
Preventing child abuse and neglect.
https://www.cdc.gov/violenceprevention/childabuseandneglect/

Child Welfare Information Gateway. (n.d.). Kinship care. U.S. Department of Health and Human Services, Administration for Children and Families, Children's Bureau. https://www.childwelfare.gov/topics/permanency/kinship-care/

Childhelp. (n.d.). National child abuse hotline. https://www.childhelp.org/hotline/

Christenson, S. L., & Reschly, A. L. (Eds.). (2010). Handbook of school-family partnerships. Routledge.

Christian, C. W.; Committee on Child Abuse and Neglect. (2015). The evaluation of suspected child physical abuse. Pediatrics, 135(5), e1337–e1354. https://doi.org/10.1542/peds.2015-0356

Cochrane. (n.d.). Kinship care for the safety, permanency, and well-being of children removed from the home for maltreatment. https://www.cochrane.org/evidence/CD006546_kinship-care-safety-permanency-and-well-being-maltreated-children

Cohen, J. A., Mannarino, A. P., & Deblinger, E. (2017). Trauma-focused CBT for children and adolescents: Treatment applications. Guilford Press.

Crisis Text Line. (n.d.). Crisis Text Line. https://www.crisistextline.org/

Darling, N., & Steinberg, L. (1993). Parenting style as context: An integrative model. Psychological Bulletin, 113(3), 487–496.

Davies, P. T., & Cummings, E. M. (1994). Marital conflict and child adjustment: An emotional security hypothesis. Psychological Bulletin, 116(3), 387–411.

Davies, P. T., Harold, G. T., Goeke-Morey, M. C., & Cummings, E. M. (2002). Child emotional security and interparental conflict. Monographs of the Society for Research in Child Development, 67(3, Serial No. 270), 1–115.

Davies, P. T., Sturge-Apple, M. L., Cicchetti, D., & Cummings, E. M. (2008). Adrenocortical underpinnings of children's psychological reactivity to interparental conflict. Child Development, 79(6), 1693–1706. https://doi.org/10.1111/j.1467-8624.2008.01219.x

Eddy, B., Burns, A. T., & Chafin, K. (2020). BIFF for Coparent Communication: Your guide to difficult texts, emails, and social media posts. Unhooked Books/High Conflict Institute Press.

Epstein, J. L. (2011). School, family, and community partnerships: Preparing educators and improving schools (2nd ed.). Westview Press.

Erel, O., & Burman, B. (1995). Interrelatedness of marital relations and parent–child relations: A meta-analytic review. Psychological Bulletin, 118(1), 108–132.

Feinberg, M. E. (2003). The internal structure and ecological context of coparenting: A framework for research and intervention. Parenting: Science and Practice, 3(2), 95–131.

Feinberg, M. E. (2003). The internal structure and ecological context of coparenting: A framework for research and intervention. Parenting: Science and Practice, 3(2), 95–131. https://doi.org/10.1207/S15327922PAR0302_01

Felitti, V. J., Anda, R. F., Nordenberg, D., et al. (1998). Relationship of childhood abuse and household dysfunction to many of the leading causes of death in adults: The Adverse Childhood Expcricnccs (ΛCE) Study. American Journal of Preventive Medicine, 14(4), 245–258.

Fivush, R., Bohanek, J. G., & Duke, M. (2008). The intergenerational self: Subjective perspective and family history. In F. Sani (Ed.), Self continuity:

Individual and collective perspectives (pp. 131–143). Psychology Press.

Gershoff, E. T., & Grogan-Kaylor, A. (2016). Spanking and child outcomes: Old controversies and new meta-analyses. Journal of Family Psychology, 30(4), 453–469. https://doi.org/10.1037/fam0000191

Gollwitzer, P. M. (1999). Implementation intentions: Strong effects of simple plans. American Psychologist, 54(7), 493–503. https://doi.org/10.1037/0003-066X.54.7.493

Gottman, J. M., & Gottman, J. S. (2017). The natural principles of love. Journal of Family Theory & Review, 9(1), 7–26. https://doi.org/10.1111/jftr.12182

Gottman, J., & DeClaire, J. (1997). Raising an emotionally intelligent child. Simon & Schuster.

Gross, J. J. (2015). Emotion regulation: Current status and future prospects. Psychological Inquiry, 26(1), 1–26. https://doi.org/10.1080/1047840X.2014.940781

Harvard University, Center on the Developing Child. (n.d.). Toxic stress. https://developingchild.harvard.edu/science/key-concepts/toxic-stress/

International Association for Suicide Prevention. (n.d.). Find a helpline. https://iasp.findahelpline.com/

Johnson, S. M. (2019). Attachment theory in practice: Emotionally focused therapy (EFT) with individuals, couples, and families. Guilford Press.

Johnston, J. R., Campbell, L. E. G., & Mayes, S. S. (1985). Latent hostility and divorce: A developmental study of children. American Journal of Orthopsychiatry, 55(4), 556–567.

Kazdin, A. E. (2005). Parent management training: Treatment for oppositional, aggressive, and antisocial behavior in children and adolescents. Oxford University Press.

Kelly, J. B., & Lamb, M. E. (2000). Using child development research to make appropriate custody and access decisions for young children. Family and Conciliation Courts Review, 38(3), 297–311.

Lally, P., van Jaarsveld, C. H. M., Potts, H. W. W., & Wardle, J. (2010). How are habits formed: Modelling habit formation in the real world. European Journal of Social Psychology, 40(6), 998–1009. https://doi.org/10.1002/ejsp.674

Lamb, M. E. (2012). Critical analysis of research on parenting plans and children's well-being. In L.

Drozd, M. Saini, & N. Olesen (Eds.), Parenting plan evaluations: Applied research for the family court (pp. 214–242). Oxford University Press.

Linehan, M. M. (2015). DBT skills training manual (2nd ed.). Guilford Press.

Maccoby, E. E., & Martin, J. A. (1983). Socialization in the context of the family: Parent–child interaction. In P. H. Mussen (Ed.), Handbook of child psychology (Vol. 4, pp. 1–101). Wiley.

Masten, A. S. (2014). Ordinary magic: Resilience in development. Guilford Press.

McAdams, D. P. (2013). The redemptive self: Stories Americans live by (Revised and expanded ed.). Oxford University Press.

McLaughlin, K. A., Sheridan, M. A., & Lambert, H. K. (2014). Childhood adversity and neural development: Deprivation and threat as distinct dimensions of early experience. Neuroscience & Biobehavioral Reviews, 47, 578–591.

Mikolajczak, M., & Roskam, I. (2018). A theoretical and clinical framework for parental burnout: The balance between risks and resources (BR2). Frontiers in Psychology, 9, 886. https://doi.org/10.3389/fpsyg.2018.00886

Mikulincer, M., & Shaver, P. R. (2016). Attachment in adulthood: Structure, dynamics, and change (2nd ed.). Guilford Press.

Minuchin, S. (1974). Families and family therapy. Harvard University Press.

National Association of School Psychologists. (2020). The school psychologist's role in promoting family–school partnerships. https://www.nasponline.org/resources-and-publications/resources-and-podcasts/family-school-partnerships

National Children's Alliance. (n.d.). Standards for accredited members / child advocacy center model. https://www.nationalchildrensalliance.org/

National Children's Alliance. (n.d.). Standards for accredited members. https://www.nationalchildrensalliance.org/

National Domestic Violence Hotline. (n.d.). Domestic violence support. https://www.thehotline.org/

National Human Trafficking Hotline. (n.d.). Contact us. https://humantraffickinghotline.org/en/contact

Nunes, C. E., de Roten, Y., El Ghaziri, N., Favez, N., & Darwiche, J. (2021). Co-parenting programs:

A systematic review and meta-analysis. Family Relations, 70(3), 759–776.

Perry, B. D., & Szalavitz, M. (2006). The boy who was raised as a dog: And other stories from a child psychiatrist's notebook. Basic Books.

Pinquart, M. (2017). Associations of parenting dimensions and styles with internalizing symptoms in children and adolescents: A meta-analysis. Marriage & Family Review, 53(7), 613–640.

Porges, S. W. (2011). The polyvagal theory: Neurophysiological foundations of emotions, attachment, communication, and self-regulation. W. W. Norton.

Porges, S. W. (2022). Polyvagal theory: A science of safety. Frontiers in Integrative Neuroscience, 16, 871227. https://doi.org/10.3389/fnint.2022.871227

RAINN. (n.d.). National sexual assault hotline. https://rainn.org/help-and-healing/hotline/

Ribas, L. H., Montezano, B. B., Nieves, M., Kampmann, L. B., & Jansen, K. (2024). The role of parental stress on emotional and behavioral problems in offspring: A systematic review with meta-analysis. Jornal de Pediatria, 100(6), 565–585. https://doi.org/10.1016/j.jped.2024.02.003

Rosanbalm, K. D., & Murray, D. W. (2017). Caregiver co-regulation across development: A practice brief (OPRE Brief #2017-80). Office of Planning, Research and Evaluation, Administration for Children and Families, U.S. Department of Health and Human Services.

Rubin, D., Springer, S. H., Zlotnik, S., Kang-Yi, C. D., & Council on Foster Care, Adoption, and Kinship Care. (2017). Needs of kinship care families and pediatric practice. Pediatrics, 139(4), e20170099. https://doi.org/10.1542/peds.2017-0099

Saini, M., Drozd, L. M., & Olesen, N. W. (2017). Parenting plan evaluations: Applied research for the family court. Oxford University Press.

Sandler, I. N., Tein, J. Y., Wolchik, S., & Ayers, T. S. (2016). The effects of the New Beginnings Program on children and adolescents. Prevention Science, 17(1), 75–86.

Sandler, I. N., Wolchik, S. A., Winslow, E., Mahrer, N. E., Moran, J. A., Weinstock, D., & Schenck, C. (2012). Quality of coparenting and child adjustment after divorce: A randomized trial. Journal of Consulting and Clinical Psychology, 80(4), 706–717

Schittek, A., Roskam, I., & Mikolajczak, M. (2024). Parental burnout stages and their link to parental violence: A longitudinal study. Journal of Applied Developmental Psychology, 95, 101717. https://doi.org/10.1016/j.appdev.2024.101717

Schrodt, P. (2025). Interparental conflict and parent–child triangulation: A meta-analytical review of children feeling caught between parents. Human Communication Research. Advance online publication. https://doi.org/10.1093/hcr/hqaf018

Sege, R. D., & Siegel, B. S.; Council on Child Abuse and Neglect; Committee on Psychosocial Aspects of Child and Family Health. (2018). Effective discipline to raise healthy children. Pediatrics, 142(6), e20183112. https://doi.org/10.1542/peds.2018-3112

Shonkoff, J. P., Garner, A. S.; Committee on Psychosocial Aspects of Child and Family Health; Committee on Early Childhood, Adoption, and Dependent Care; Section on Developmental and Behavioral Pediatrics. (2012). The lifelong effects of early childhood adversity and toxic stress. Pediatrics, 129(1), e232–e246. https://doi.org/10.1542/peds.2011-2663

Siegel, D. J. (2012). The developing mind: How relationships and the brain interact to shape who we are (2nd ed.). Guilford Press.

Siegel, D. J., & Bryson, T. P. (2011). The Whole-Brain Child: 12 revolutionary strategies to nurture your child's developing mind. Bantam.

Substance Abuse and Mental Health Services Administration. (2014). SAMHSA's concept of trauma and guidance for a trauma-informed approach (HHS Publication No. SMA14-4884). https://store.samhsa.gov/product/SAMHSA-s-Concept-of-Trauma-and-Guidance-for-a-Trauma-Informed-Approach/SMA14-4884

Substance Abuse and Mental Health Services Administration. (2014). SAMHSA's concept of trauma and guidance for a trauma-informed approach (HHS Publication No. SMA14-4884). https://store.samhsa.gov/product/SMA14-4884

Substance Abuse and Mental Health Services Administration. (n.d.). 988 Suicide & Crisis Lifeline. https://www.samhsa.gov/mental-health/988

The Trevor Project. (n.d.). Here for you 24/7: How to reach out to The Trevor Project. https://www.thetrevorproject.org/resources/guide/here-for-you-24-7-how-to-reach-out-to-the-trevor-project/

van der Kolk, B. A. (2014). The body keeps the score: Brain, mind, and body in the healing of trauma. Viking.

van Eldik, W. M., Luijk, M. P. C. M., Parry, L. Q., & Prinzie, P. (2020). The interparental relationship: Meta-analytic associations with children's maladjustment and responses to interparental conflict. Psychological Bulletin, 146(7), 553–594. https://doi.org/10.1037/bul0000233

Winokur, M., Holtan, A., & Batchelder, K. E. (2018). Systematic review of kinship care effects on safety, permanency, and well-being outcomes. Research on Social Work Practice, 28(1), 19–32. https://doi.org/10.1177/1049731515620843

Wolff, J. C., & Ollendick, T. H. (2006). The comorbidity of conduct problems and depression in childhood and adolescence. Clinical Psychology Review, 26(1), 1–17.

World Health Organization. (2020). INSPIRE: Seven strategies for ending violence against children. https://www.who.int/publications/i/item/97892400 21024

About the Author

Cindy H. Carr, D.Min., MACL lives in Harrisonburg, Virginia, and has spent over forty years working in ministry and business, helping people navigate change, conflict, and growth with wisdom and steadiness. One of her deepest passions has been building strong families—especially in seasons when relationships are strained and children need adults to lead well.

As a pastor and pastoral counselor, Dr. Carr has devoted years to research, teaching, and hands-on ministry focused on family systems, emotional regulation, and child-centered care. Her work brings together practical tools, grounded faith, and real-world experience to help caregivers protect children from adult conflict while creating homes marked by stability, dignity, and repair.

Learn more about Cindy and her work at **CindyHCarr.com**